a Clia

HISTORY THROUGH STAMPS

HISTORY THROUGH STAMPS

A Survey of Modern World History

DAVID KEEP

DAVID & CHARLES

NEWTON ABBOT   LONDON

NORTH POMFRET (VT)   VANCOUVER

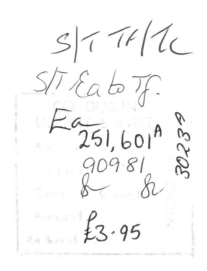
0 7153 6576 2

© David Keep 1974

Set in 10 on 11pt Times by Trade Linotype Ltd Birmingham and printed in Great Britain by Biddles Limited Guildford for David & Charles (Holdings) Limited South Devon House Newton Abbot Devon

Published in the United States of America by   David & Charles Inc   North Pomfret Vermont   05053   USA

Published in Canada by Douglas David & Charles Limited 3645 McKechnie Drive West Vancouver BC

CONTENTS

LIST OF ILLUSTRATIONS

PLATES

IN THE TEXT

can be made up of short sets of definitives

ACKNOWLEDGEMENTS

The author is grateful to Stanley Gibbons Ltd, London, for photographs of the following stamps: 20, 51, 76, 89, 307, 316 and 458. Thanks are also due to many dealers who have helped to find odd examples, and above all to my wife, who mounted the stamps and checked the manuscript with patience and skill.

INTRODUCTION

Cheap, international postage was the child of steam transport and became the handmaid of the expansion of trade and education in the nineteenth century. Postage stamps rapidly became a means of expressing independence, or asserting sovereignty. They have been used by governments in exile (201–5). Agencies have provided them for tiny states, to the financial advantage of both (423–4). Some unscrupulous dealers have provided sets for fictitious governments. Children are attracted by pictorial themes, and as the prospect of collecting the 165,000 or so stamps so far produced becomes impossible, collectors soon move to either thematic collecting or to the stamps of their own country. This has been the practice in the USA and the USSR for a long time. Since the rapid increase in stamp issues and the opening of the Philatelic Bureau in the sixties, collecting in Britain has tended to follow the same pattern, with dealers who only stock British stamps.

This book is intended to renew interest in general collecting. By showing how stamps are related to modern history, it is possible to trace the development of nationalism within Europe up to 1919 and the parallel spread of colonial empires. The spread of fascism and then of communism may be seen in the artistic style and symbolism of stamp designs. The rapid political transformation of Africa and Asia, which is still taking place, can be shown by the changes in the names and styles of the former colonies. An historical collection can be made up of short sets of definitive stamps with no need to aim at completion, since short-lives issues, like the Edward VII 6d IR Official, and high values make this a costly process (76).

Childhood or cheap general collections form a good basis for this sort of collection, and the author has looked through a good many in the course of selecting the stamps for the plates. The idea for this book arose from the purchase of a Stanley Gibbons *Ideal* album with spaces for every stamp up to 1914. There are plenty of pre-war printed albums on the market, and older readers will remember how much history and geography they assimilated from such albums without any conscious effort. There is a danger that today's children will have more restricted horizons and that their parents will overlook important political developments in the third world. Definitive stamps, even if confined to one for each ruler, will help to identify the nature of the regime, and say something about the economy.

The illustrations in this book, then, are a rapid guide to the history of the past 150 years. Overprints and surcharges are of great historical interest as they always arise from an emergency. Coronations and jubilees have an obvious place as do the memorial issues for statesmen, since it is a common convention not to portray living men, so that the cult of personality which has been so disruptive to democracies may be guarded against. It may well be that readers will do no more than look more carefully at their foreign mail or put a few interesting stamps away in a stock-book or printed album like the Stanley Gibbons *Strand*, now in its thirty-third edition. Others may like to build up an extensive but inexpensive general collection. This will appeal to confirmed stamp collectors who have reached the stage with their special interests where any addition involves writing cheques. A new world collection might develop one area or period at a time and will certainly, by definition, prove to be a lifelong interest.

In such a collection, the value of the stamps is completely secondary to their design. Collectors whose prime concern is value, have become very finicky about condition. Classic, that is pre-1870 issues, have increased greatly in price in fine condition but it is still not difficult to find cut copies at less than 10 per cent of catalogue value—the unique one cent black-on-magenta British Guiana is cut (307).

It is illustrated in this book and collectors have to be content with its photograph, but the British rule could just as well be represented by any of the arms of the colony designs which were in use in 1852–1934. Sometimes a heavy postmark may add to the information which appears on the stamp, and so be preferable to a lightly used copy. The earliest British colonial stamps can only be distinguished by the form of cancellation. Many nineteenth-century designs were in use for a long time; forty years in the case of the first British stamp (29). A damaged piece of evidence is better than none at all and historians will not despise reprints and remainders, especially if they were made from the original plates (30).

Many of the illustrations in this book are cheap stamps, that is, catalogued by Gibbons at a nominal handling charge of five pence. This is not to say that they are common, for though no doubt countless old collections exist, smaller quantities were used than today and very few dealers stock foreign stamps. This adds excitement to the search, which will include children's packets in chain stores. If interest in general collecting revives, no doubt dealers will give their attention to it again. The virtue of each collector setting his own norms is that he can use any material he chooses, and include anything which he finds particularly attractive. The appeal of stamps should in any case be their intrinsic beauty rather than their computed and even

deliberate scarcity. There is great satisfaction in making an attractive and interesting stamp collection from discarded envelopes. If this can be organised, as when former pupils send foreign stamps to schools or packets are purchased from missionary societies, young people can find added excitement in sorting them out. Children have only followed their parents in collecting taste, and there is every educational justification for reversing the obsession with value and replacing it with an interest in the content. If we do not study what we collect, we are no better than the Victorian country child with her hoard of old buttons—which she could not even count.

This book is a brief survey of modern world history illustrated by stamps. These have been selected to make important points about the country involved, and could have been increased tenfold without difficulty. There is an obvious bias towards Europe and the two world wars of this century, with the stamps of Germany naturally prominent; but this is a period of history that we still neglect at our peril and that will awaken half-memories in older readers. Politics in Africa is tending to

PLATE 1
Communication

Steam transport made cheap international post possible. Although airmails have replaced steam in the past fifty years, the railway and the postal system often developed together. This plate shows an alternative approach to history in stamps, through anniversary issues.

The Spread of World Railways
1 Germany 1835
2 Finland 1862
3 Holland 1839
4 Switzerland 1847
5 Brazil 1854
6 South Africa 1860
7 British India 1861
8 New Zealand 1863
9 British West Africa 1903

PLATE 1

1

2

3

4

5

6

7

8

9

echo that of the Balkans in the nineteenth century, and some collectors might like to start where this work finishes and begin a collection with the independence of Ghana (366). Similarly, it has only been possible within the present scope to show a few of the islands of the West Indies and the Pacific and anyone with cultural ties to these areas could develop collections. A third area of new interest is in the stamps for international agencies (10–19).

Many of the stamps shown here portray rulers, national coats-of-arms, or idealised workers in communist states and the democracies which the victors in 1946 created out of the defeated powers (131–3, 214, 225). There are some examples of pictorial stamps which reproduce paintings or photographs, but in this work these are not regarded as primary evidence. A few are included in the USA but if commemorative issues were used throughout, this book would become an outline of world history from the invention of cave paintings! The stamps are treated as official documents which make a statement about the system of government and the currency and its purchasing power. This can be deduced from the current postage rate, which is itself a great help in cataloguing undated special issues. In the USA, for example, the rate was 4c in 1958, 5c in 1963, 6c in 1968 and 8c in 1971. This is to treat stamp collecting on a par with collecting coins rather than medals, or with those commercially produced discs which are designed for collectors. Many stamps, especially from tiny states, come into this category. The collector who concentrates on postally used items has the unique advantage of being able to have his cake and eat it, as the used stamp has already fulfilled its purpose! Definitive stamps become a means of illustrating contemporary history from their own tiny, but precise, designs.

PLATE 2
International Co-operation

10 The Universal Postal Union was set up in 1874 to facilitate the movement of mail. Some American countries recorded their membership on every issue in the last years of the nineteenth century, as on this 1896 Salvador design. Most of the world marked its seventy-fifth anniversary in 1949 (57).
11 The International Court of Justice arose from the Hague Conference on disarmament in 1901. It issued stamps from 1934.
12 The League of Nations followed the Red Cross by setting up its headquarters in Geneva 1920–46. It overprinted Swiss stamps.
13 The International Labour Office 1919, became a part of the League and UNO. This design replaced overprints in 1956.
14 The Swiss PTT issued stamps for the other agencies of the UN—a 1958 design for the International Education Office.
15 The Swiss PTT issued general stamps for the old Geneva headquarters 1950–3, when the UN took over with its own designs.
16 USA 1962. Memorial issue for Dag Hammerskjöld, secretary-general of the UN 1953–61, who died in a Congo air crash.
17 UN New York 1972, to mark the important non-proliferation of nuclear weapons treaty.
18 The seal of the UN on the first set 1951
19 New York 1965: aerial view of the building

This, then, is not another book of postal history, nor in a sense is it primarily about stamps. The text could just as well have been illustrated by coins, postcards or pictures selected from the press. The thesis is that stamps are by their very nature interesting, and the plates should appeal as much to those who have never collected as to those who are addicts of this most convenient and widely accessible hobby, which need cost nothing yet can take a fortune. The postage stamp does have some advantages as an illus-

PLATE 2

10

11

12

13

14

15

16

17

18

19

INTRODUCTION

tration since it can contain more detail than a coin and is more readily displayed than a photograph. It became used as a means of propaganda, some of which is good, like the publication of the revived Olympic ideal (21–8) or the propagation of the Freedom from Hunger Campaign.

Shortage of space has limited one large, complementary area. Postal stationery appeared in the form of the Mulready envelope issued with the first stamps. There have been times when no alternative has been available, as in the rare cover from Mecca illustrated (20) or in the prisoner-of-war cards which are still precious mementoes to some families. These contrast with the artificiality of first-day covers.

20 (below) Interim cover posted at Mecca 4 December 1916, issued between the expulsion of the Turks by the Arabs (aided by T. E. Lawrence) and the first stamps for Hejaz in 1916.

PLATE 3
International Sport

Pierre de Coubertin (28) re-established the Olympic Games in Greece in 1896 to foster friendship and co-operation. An Olympiad is counted each four years, whether games are held or not.

21 The first Olympiad, Athens 1896
22 VII Olympiad, Antwerp 1920
23 VIII Olympiad, Paris 1924
24 IX Olympiad, Los Angeles 1928
25 XIV Olympiad 1948, winter sports at St Moritz, Switzerland
26 XIV Olympiad, London 1948
27 XVI Olympiad, Melbourne 1956
28 First series 1968, for the XX Olympiad at Munich 1972. It has become common to issue several sets each time.

PLATE 3

21

22

23

24

25

26

27

28

CHAPTER ONE
EUROPE 1830-1917

Great Britain issued the world's first postage stamp in the fourth year of Victoria's reign (29). When her uncle's portrait followed in 1849, he was in the nineteenth year of his reign as first king of the Belgians (59). Victoria's Europe in 1840 was very much that of the Congress of Vienna in 1815, which had undone as much of the work of Napoleon as it could. Revolutions in 1830 had split Belgium and the Netherlands, which had been united as a buffer against France, and had established a liberal monarchy in France. Europe was still ruled by kings, many of them claiming absolute power. But there were also many princes and archdukes of minor states. Germany and Italy only existed as ideas, though they had a taste of union under Napoleon. Andorra (161), Luxemburg (52–5), Monaco (74–5), and San Marino (69), together with the Vatican City (194), have maintained their independence.

There are three main issues in nineteenth-century European history. The first is the rapid spread of industry in Britain, then Belgium and Germany; at the same time the population increased rapidly (1–4). (The need for markets and materials stimulated the growth of empires, as described in chapter four.) The second is nationalism, the desire of people linked by language and culture to be united. So Greece was freed from Turkey (101), Belgium from Holland, Norway from Sweden (39–43), and Eire from Britain (158–60). The national struggles of the races of East Europe created the third problem, the breaking up of the great Ottoman Empire (102), which had threatened Austria, Spain and Persia. This brought Austria and Russia into conflict. In

PLATE 4
The House of Windsor

The Elector of Hanover became king of England in 1714. The family name was changed to Windsor in World War I.

29 Victoria, 1837–1901, became the model for public morality and after her jubilee a symbol of benevolent power. The 'penny black', 1840, was the world's first stamp.

30 Heligoland was British 1810–90; it was ceded to the German Empire. Most stamps are reprints.

31 Gibraltar became British in 1713, though it is claimed by Spain. It used Spanish currency 1889–1903. Since then it has used British.

32 Edward VII, 1901–10, acceded to the throne aged sixty. His reign brought back colour into public life, together with the display of Britain's hard-earned wealth.

33 George V, 1910–36, was born in 1865. The first British commemorative stamp shows him as emperor, but the lion was already at bay. He extended the royal public service.

34 Edward VIII, 1936, abdicated in order to marry the Duchess of Windsor. He died in 1972.

35 George VI, 1936–52, and Elizabeth the Queen Mother, at their coronation 1937

36 Their silver-wedding portrait of 1948

37 Elizabeth II, queen since 6 February 1952. The silver-wedding portrait with Philip, Duke of Edinburgh 1972

38 Charles, proclaimed Prince of Wales 1969.

PLATE 4

29

30

31

32

33

34

35

36

37

38

1916 Charles, the last Habsburg, assumed an uneasy throne for two years (96). With his abdication, Vienna became a capital with no king and almost no territory. In 1917 the last of the Romanovs was murdered (99), and a new kind of government came into being which has radically altered world politics. The Russian revolution and the arrival of American troops in Europe were even more the end of the nineteenth century than the peace of 1919.

Monarchy has survived in northern Europe because political change came slowly and by the consent of the rulers. Industry increased the rich middle classes, who wanted free trade for their goods, a share in government and more education for themselves. Their appeal to the idea of democracy extended this to all adults. In Britain this took from 1832 to 1928, with similar steady progress in Scandinavia and the Low Countries, and Switzerland (56–8). State education, health and pensions have continued to develop. The crown has continued as a national symbol, able to mediate between parties (as George V did in 1911 in the conflict over the power of the House of Lords) and to provide glamour and colour. Thus it plays an important part in public life. Elected heads of state without this aura are often overlooked by the people. If they have great power, the processes of election and security become more costly than royal families.

The British post office did not issue any pictorial or commemorative stamps until 1924, but the increasing colonial issues show the world importance of the British navy. The Ionian Islands were British until 1864, and Heligoland until 1890 (30). Britain and France fought Russia 1854–6 to protect Turkey. As a reward for diplomatic help at Berlin in 1878, Cyprus (103) was added to Gibraltar (31) and Malta (235) in the Mediterranean. After the purchase of the Suez Canal in 1875 (324) this was the strategic route to India and the life-line of the British empire.

The jubilees of 1887 and 1897 (281) were the heyday of British power. The queen's grandson was emperor of Germany from 1888. Granddaughters were married to the future rulers of Russia (99) and Rumania (152). London was the biggest, brightest and richest city in the world. The jubilee poem 'Recessional' by Rudyard Kipling warned of the responsibility of power. The Boer war was a shock (348), but the gay summer of Edward VII left Britain unprepared for the strikes and civil unrest which preceded world war. The war at first produced enthusiastic response from the empire (84–7) but after 1916 it required conscription, rationing and a rigidly planned economy.

PLATE 5
North-European Monarchies

Norway was united with Denmark until 1814 and ruled by the king of Sweden until 1905.
39 Haakon VII 1905–57, a Danish prince, was an exile in London 1940–45 (201).
40 Olav V 21 September 1957

Sweden issued this first portrait in 1885, though Oscar I appeared on Norway in 1856.
41 Oscar II 1872–1907
42 Gustav V 1907–50, aged eighty, 1938
43 Gustav VI Adolf 1950–73

Denmark replaced numeral designs in 1904.
44 Christian IX 1863–1906
45 Frederick VIII 1906–12
46 Christian X 1912–47. Portrait of 1942 during the German occupation
47 Frederick IX 1947–72, who has been succeeded by his daughter Margrethe.

The Netherlands are still ruled by the House of Orange, descended from William the Silent.
48 William III 1849–90, on the 1864 issue
49 Wilhelmina 1890–1948, came to the throne aged ten, portrayed in 1898. Another wartime exile in London, she lived until 1962 (202, 481).
50 Juliana became queen on her mother's abdication in 1948 (312). The 1969 definitive.

PLATE 5

39

40

41

42

43

44

45

46

47

48

49

50

The nineteenth century was still an age of heroes, however, and the unification of Italy is romantic and exciting. The idea was fostered by writers like Mazzini, and journals like *Il Risorgimento* founded by the future prime minister of Piedmont in 1847. But it was the co-operation of Cavour and Victor Emmanuel II with the guerrilla Garibaldi which made the Italian peninsula into a single state. The classic stamps show Italy in 1815 (65–6). Lombardy and Venice were ruled by Austria (64), Rome and the small states round it came under the rule of the pope (66), though it depended on Napoleon III for protection. In 1846 Pius IX had been a progressive, but the revolutions of 1848 and fears for the power of the church led to the reactionary council of 1870. When the king occupied Rome in 1871, the popes became prisoners until Pius XI made the Lateran Treaty in 1929 (194).

Beside these special areas there were two kingdoms and four principalities. 'Bomba', the hated king of the two Sicilies died in 1859, between the issue of stamps for Naples and Sicily. In 1860 Garibaldi landed with his thousand redshirts, defeated the Neapolitan army and hailed Victor Emmanuel as king of Italy. The Sardinian stamp was modified for Naples, and then united Italy (65). Tuscany, Parma, Modena and Romagna were absorbed in 1859 and the Italian lands added in 1866 after the war between Austria and Prussia.

This seems to be an adventure with a happy ending. Britain, France and Germany were friendly, Rome was rebuilt as a fine capital, and an empire started in Africa (347). But the conflict with the church made politics radical and unstable, and the difference between the industrial north and the poor south continued. Italy formed the Triple Alliance with Germany and Austria in 1882, but joined Britain and France in 1915 for the price of Trieste.

The revolutions of 1848 which brought Victor Emmanuel to the throne, destroyed the monarchy in France. The Second Republic

51 (above) Genevan cantonal issue of 1843 cut as a vertical instead of horizontal pair, which in 1972 realised £22,000.

PLATE 6
Luxemburg, Switzerland and Belgium

Luxemburg, a medieval Grand Duchy which has survived as an industrial state in the EEC. Ruled by the king of Holland until 1890 (48).
52 Adolf of Nassau 1890–1905
53 William IV 1905–12
54 Marie Adelaide 1912–19
55 Charlotte 1919–64

Switzerland, cantonal stamps appeared in 1843.
56 The first federal design of 1850
57 The twenty-fifth anniversary of the UPU (10), which has its office in Bern.
58 International Disarmament Conference, Geneva 1932 (12–15)

Belgium was separated from Holland in 1831.
59 Leopold I 1831–65, revised design 1849
60 Leopold II 1865–1909 (336–7). The labels discouraged posting on Sundays from 1893 to 1914. The 1905 portrait
61 Albert I, 1909–34, the war hero in trench dress on the victory design 1919–20
62 Leopold III 1934–51
63 Baudouin 17 July 1951. His father abdicated when he became twenty-one.

PLATE 6

52

53

54

55

56

57

58

59

60

61

62

63

began to issue stamps with the portrait of Ceres, the Roman goddess of harvest (71). The regime was short lived, though, as it chose the nephew of the great Napoleon as head of state (72). He soon adopted his uncle's title, and though he has been written off as a poor shadow, he gave France eighteen years glory. He was the hero of the Crimea, the champion of Italy against Austria in 1859, and the creator of a spacious new Paris. He could not check the unusual population decline, nor move the iron and coal mines on the German frontier. He expected Prussia to defeat Austria in 1866, but did not allow for the speed of the army which overthrew France in 1870–1 and added Alsace–Lorraine to Germany.

The mob set up communes in besieged Paris which were destroyed by the French army. The Third Republic turned to empire-building to cover its shame, with the symbols of Peace and Commerce (73). General Boulanger threatened a coup in 1889–90, and the Dreyfus affair 1894–1906 showed up national divisions. In 1907 close co-operation with Russia and Britain was developed from their fear of Germany. This appeared to offer security, but meant that France was drawn into a Balkan war in 1914.

Until 1870 the German peoples were united only by language and the fiction of the Holy Roman Empire. Napoleon had abolished this in 1806; but it was restored in 1815 and its wily Chancellor Metternich (who fell in the liberal eruption of 1848) controlled Europe. The German parliaments were overthrown and the vigorous Francis Joseph (90–2) set out to maintain the Habsburg power.

The empire was increasingly rivalled by industrialised Prussia, which had built up a northern customs union by 1844 and made Berlin the centre of German railways. In 1862 Bismarck became chief minister, determined to unite Germany. He defeated Denmark in 1864, and the combined forces of Austria and the smaller German states at the battle of Sadowa in 1866. Bremen, Brunswick (79),

Hamburg, Lubeck, Mecklenburg, Oldenburg and Saxony joined Prussia in the North-German Confederation in 1868. Hungary became a separate state under Francis Joseph as king (92), and the empire turned its back on Germany, seeking consolation in the east. The southern Slav provinces of Bosnia-Herzegovinia were taken from Turkey in 1878, despite their affinity with Serbia (97, 109).

PLATE 7
The Unification of Italy and France

64 Austrian Italy: the final design of 1864 before union with Italy in 1866
65 Sardinia 1855, Victor Emmanuel II 1849–78. He became the focal point for the creation of a single state.
66 Roman States 1852–68. Typographed for use under the rule of Pope Pius IX, until Rome was included in the new kingdom in 1870.
67 Victor Emmanuel II as king of Italy 1865
68 Humbert I 1878–1900
69 San Marino, the only independent state after 1870, celebrated the Italian victory in World War I.
70 Victor Emmanuel III 1900–44, in the 1906 portrait. The king who set up and overthrew fascism. He abdicated in favour of Humbert II, who reigned until 1946.

France
71 The 1848 revolution set up the Second Republic, which adopted Ceres as the symbol for its stamps in 1849. This perforated form is from the Third Republic re-issue of 1870.
72 Napoleon III as the president replaced Ceres in 1852. He became emperor in 1853.
73 Peace and Commerce, the first of a series of republican symbols, epitomise the classic ideals of the age of trade and empire.

Monaco, another surviving city-state.
74 Prince Albert 1889–1922, in 1910—an uncommon example of postage-due portrait
75 Louis II 1922–49

PLATE 7

64

65

66

67

68

69

70

71

72

73

74

75

Bismarck was not able to unite the rest of Germany while France was a threat. The death of Isabella II of Spain (114) led to conflict, and France declared war in 1870. By 1871 only Paris and irregular forces were left, and William of Prussia was proclaimed German emperor (80). In deference to his fellow kings, Bismarck had imperial stamps printed with numerals or symbols. He was dominant until 1890.

William II, the grandson of Queen Victoria, set out to establish a world empire and a navy to rival the British. The launching of *Dreadnought* in 1906 meant a costly new start. It is ironic that aircraft-carriers rendered the battleship obsolete before any major battle took place. The emperor supported the Boers (348) and his aggressive stance in North Africa drove Britain and France closer.

By 1912 Britain and Germany had drifted into a dangerous rivalry, while France wanted the return of Alsace–Lorraine. Germany had the Schlieffen plan ready—which would circumvent the Maginot Line by invading Belgium. Britain and France were holding joint staff discussions. The real danger lay in the east, however.

Russia was outwardly strong and aggressive. Finland (98), Poland and the Baltic States were part of the tsar's empire, and until the war with Japan in 1904, increasing areas of Asia were absorbed. In the west, she acted as champion of all the slav peoples, and was determined to win control of the Bosphorus and access to the Mediterranean. Her modest stamps gave no hint of this, nor of her military defeat in the Crimea in 1856 and her diplomatic check at Berlin in 1878. Revolution in 1905 was followed by inadequate reform, and in 1914 an ill-prepared Russia met the forces of Germany and Austria–Hungary.

76 (top right) The rarest British stamp, now worth £12,000, is the 6d dull-purple Inland Revenue Official, issued on 14 March 1904, the day that the use of separate official stamps ceased.

PLATE 8
The Rise of Germany and World War I

77 Bavaria was second to Prussia in Germany, but deprived of Austrian support, became a kingdom within the Reich in 1871. Ludwig III 1914–18, was followed by soviet republic.

78 Brunswick 1857: joined the North-German Confederation under Prussia in 1868.

79 Württemberg 1856, also a monarchy until 1918

80 The German Empire: William I of Prussia, 1861–88 was proclaimed at Versailles in 1871.

81 The yacht *Hohenzollern* of William II, 1888–1918, which after 1900 appeared on the stamps of the rapidly gained overseas empire.

82 The Schlieffen plan of 1914 involved the invasion of neutral Belgium to reach France.

83 1918 overprint for Rumania. Similar issues were made for Poland, and eastern and western commands.

The British Empire at War
The British post office did not recognise the war in any way, but most colonies raised funds and sent troops to defend Britain.

84 Canada 1915

85 Newfoundland 1919: each value indicates a battle or honours the Royal Naval Reserve.

86 Ceylon 1918: a typical colonial issue

87 Australia, 1935, remembered Gallipoli

The Cost of War

88 Belgian charity issue of 1923

PLATE 8

77

78

79

80

81

82

83

84

85

86

87

88

Plate 10 plots the breakdown of the Ottoman empire and the emergence of new states in the Balkans. The wars of 1912–13 drove Turkey from Europe and created independent Albania. The Balkans appeared to be settled by the Treaty of Bucharest, but a network of secret treaties made any conflict dangerous. The Serbs wanted union with their cousins in the Austrian empire. The Czechs and Slovaks also wanted independence, so that when a student assassinated the Austrian heir (97), Austria decided to humiliate Serbia, who could not accept all the punitive demands made on her. Austria declared war on 28 July 1914. Russia followed to protect Serbia, Germany to protect Austria, and France in support of Russia. The invasion of Belgium brought in Great Britain. A minor incident thus escalated into a major conflict which was to transform the politics and the map of Europe, and to make the USA into the leading world power.

The Germans advanced rapidly into Belgium but were checked by the 'contemptible little army' of Britain (82). There followed four years of murderous battles in which the attacker lost far more than the defender, and which drained the best young men of the three powers. The Germans broke through in the spring of 1918, but unrestricted submarine warfare and national sympathy had brought the USA into the war, and the Germans were pushed back. The armistice of 1918 was signed in the same carriage as the French had used in 1871. Versailles was again the venue for the peace conference in 1919.

In the east, Russia made some progress but apart from an offensive against Austria in 1916, was driven back in defence. There was no shortage of manpower, but organisation and transport broke down (100) and in 1917 men began to go home. Strikes and riots in March led to a provisional government and the tsar was persuaded to abdicate (99, 127–30).

Britain had failed to break through at Gallipoli in 1915–16 (87), and despite the

89 (above) A block of the first stamp for the Russian Grand Duchy of Finland in 1854. In 1972 it was sold for £15,000.

PLATE 9
The Eastern Empires

Austria–Hungary
90 Francis Joseph I 1848–1916, in 1867
91 Diamond Jubilee issue 1908
92 In 1867 Hungary achieved separate administration under Francis Joseph as king.
93 1915 charity for war-widows and orphans
94 1916–17 Hungarian war charity
95 1919 Rumanian occupation of Transylvania
96 Charles I 1916–18, abdicated in defeat.
97 1917 issue for Bosnia and Herzegovina to establish a memorial for the assassinated Archduke Franz Ferdinand, whose death at Sarajevo sparked off the war with Serbia.

The Russian Empire
98 Finland 1875. Poland had only one stamp issued in 1860.
99 Nicholas II 1894–1917, the first Russian portrait on the Romanov tercentenary set 1913
100 Economic collapse as much as military defeat led to the revolution. In 1915 three values were printed on card authorised on the back for use as silver coins.

PLATE 9

90

91

92

93

94

95

96

97

98

99

100

initial success of Serbia, there was no real allied progress until the Bulgarians broke at Salonica and the Austrians at Vittorio Veneto at the end of 1918. At the same time Allenby defeated the Turks in Palestine (395).

The war cost $7\frac{1}{4}$ million soldiers, and twice as many civilians, 6 million of these died from influenza. The rate of slaughter was the fastest the world has known—it created a terrible sense of disillusionment in Europe. The nineteenth century had seen a remarkable revival of religion among the new middle-class, evangelical in England and pietist on the continent. Protestant and Catholic missions made rapid progress in Africa, and persevered in Asia, dreaming of a Christian world by 1920. There were very close cultural relationships among the educated, as the novels of E. M. Forster and D. H. Lawrence show. The Socialist International had optimistically said that working men would not fight each other.

Five great empires went to war in 1914, and of these, only a chastened Britain survived. It was nominally greater after 1919, but the age of confident imperialism was past and the sense of 'the white man's burden' increased. Russia had fallen to bolshevik revolutionaries. In Hungary and Germany a similar fate threatened. Military defeat ended the power of the kings in Germany. Austrian Czechs had fought in France and Russia to defeat the fatherland (186–8). The USA president, Wilson, made his famous 'Fourteen Points' on the aims of the war in January 1918, and these became the basis for the peace and the formation of the League of Nations (12). International morality on the principles of open agreements, free trade, and national self-determination was to be practised. Armaments would be reduced, and war outlawed. This was a noble ideal, but it overlooked the human propensity to make the wrong choice and failed to devise an international police. It was far less successful than Metternich's Congress System, which opened the nineteenth century and gave Europe peace and progress.

PLATE 10
The Eastern Question

Russia began to encroach on the weakened Ottoman empire in the eighteenth century. After 1815 Austria and Britain supported Turkey, and attempted to set up regimes free of Russian control in emancipated states.

101 Greece became fully independent in 1833 and used Hermes as its symbol 1861–96 (20).

102 Turkey: Sultan Abdul-Hamid II 1876–1909

103 The Congress of Berlin in 1878 met under Bismarck to resettle the balance of power. Britain took Cyprus in return for her support. The first definitive in 1881

104 British post offices were set up in the Levant 1885–1921: the 1911 issue.

105 French post offices operated 1885–1923.

106 Austrian post offices operated in the Turkish Empire 1867–1914: the 1883 issue.

107 German post offices 1884–1908. Germany aimed to build a railway to Baghdad. Turkey became an ally against Russia and Britain.

108 Montenegro was an independent mountain-kingdom on the Adriatic. Nicholas became king in 1860 and granted a constitution in 1905. It became part of the new Yugoslavia in 1919.

109 Serbia gained full independence in 1878, though autonomous from 1830. Obrenovich IV 1868–89 (Milan) whose successor was murdered in 1903 by Karageorgevich.

110 Peter I 1903–21, first king of Yugoslavia

111 Bulgaria gained an exarch in 1870, and autonomy after the atrocities of 1875–6. In 1885 it seized Eastern Roumelia, and under Ferdinand of Saxe–Coburg 1887–1918 (died 1950) became a German ally. (King Boris (155))

112 Rumania won autonomy in 1862 and independence in 1877. Carol I 1866–1914 left a neutral policy, but in 1916 and 1918 Rumania joined the allies and gained Transylvania and Bessarabia from Hungary (95).

PLATE 10

101

102

103

104

105

106

107

108

109

110

111

112

CHAPTER TWO

EUROPE 1917-1973

Spain and Portugal share with Sweden and Switzerland the distinction of remaining neutral in both world wars. This is remarkable in view of their past history as great empires, but the loss of their American colonies in the fifteen years after Waterloo helped to turn their interest to internal affairs. These did, however, reflect the politics of the time.

Until the nineteenth century the Catholic Church was virtually unopposed in the peninsula, but socialist ideas then challenged the traditional rulers and the traditional culture, and both countries became republics. The Portuguese king fell in 1910 (123), when a secular state was set up. The Spanish republic lasted under three years (115), but left a split in the country which re-opened during the revived republic of 1931 (118). Portugal followed the pattern of central Europe and became a dictatorship in 1926. The system of Salazar survived to 1974.

113 (below) Pius XI (pope 1922–39) and Alfonso XIII, issued for the catacombs restoration fund.

Portugal is still the last European power with an African empire (362) but its colonial policy is changing.

Spain issued very beautiful stamps from

PLATE 11
Spain and Portugal

Spain
114 Isabella II 1833–68, in 1867. Her death led to the second Carlist war of succession.
115 Republic 1873–5: the figure of justice
116 Alfonso XII 1875–86 defeated Charles VII the pretender, whom the pope supported.
117 Alfonso XIII 1886–1931, died 1941, on the 1889 design shared with the Spanish colonies.
118 Republic 1931–8, honoured past liberals
119 De la Cierva 1895–1936 and the autogyro (forerunner of the helicopter) on the 1939 s'
120 General Franco was proclaimed 'Chi of the Spanish State' after the Moroccan arm revolted in 1936. German air support gav him victory in 1939, when this stamp appeared.

Portugal
121 Luiz 1861–89
122 Carlos 1889–1908
123 Manuel 1908–10 fled to London.
124 Ceres as symbol of the republic 1912
125 Salazar was dictator 1932–72, and adopted a fascist constitution in 1933. This 1935 slogan 'All for the Nation' is one of the few stamps that reflect modern events rather than the past.
126 1953: knight replaced the caravel of 1943.

PLATE 11

114

115

116

117

118

119

120

121

122

123

124

125

126

1905 to the fall of Alfonso XIII (118), including a long set in 1928 with the king next to Pope Pius XI (113). The country was governed by Primo de Rivera as dictator from 1923 to 1930. When the left won they restored free elections in 1931. The king fled.

The new republic was bitterly divided between the radical rule of Azana, and the pro-clerical party of Gil Robles. When Azana's popular front was re-elected in 1936 with a more radical programme, the army revolted. A bitter war followed, with both sides committing atrocities, but it was help from Mussolini and Hitler which gave Franco victory, with the Luftwaffe perfecting *blitzkreig*. Russia helped the left, but was too far away. International volunteers fought on both sides, as described by Hemingway. Their experience helped to break down pacifist feeling in the liberal countries and has left a nostalgic, and not altogether justified, sympathy for the political liberty of the defeated republic.

Scarce surcharged stamps marked the course of the war—Asturias and Leon were isolated. The republic marked its second anniversary, and the defence of Madrid, but definitive stamps marked the success of the right, and by 1939 Franco was dictator. As a client of Hitler he was very unpopular in the forties, but the setting up of American bases and the enormous expansion of tourism has made the regime less restrictive and more popular.

The Spanish civil war was the overture to World War II. Europe had never been freed from the tensions left from the earlier war. The revolution in Russia in 1917 had led to a provisional government under the liberal Kerensky (127). The German army smuggled the bolshevik leader, Lenin, from Switzerland. He organised a force which overthrew the interim regime in Petrograd, renamed Leningrad, in the 'October' revolution. The communists then issued the symbolic 'breaking of the fetters' stamp (128).

It took five years to establish the new government and to rebuild a sound currency and postal service (129). Trotsky made the humiliating treaty of Brest–Litovsk on 3 March 1918, after a further German advance. A bitter civil war broke out, recorded by surcharged stamps and the crude relief issues for the Volga and Rostov-on-Don. The red army put up a heroic resistance to the trained, but divided, whites. Their stamps are now rare, but issues appeared for Kolchak's government in Siberia 1918–20 (187). Japan helped to maintain white control of Vladivostok until 1922. In the south there were stamps for the Kuban and Don cossacks, and the Dennikin and Wrangel governments in the Crimea (137). Britain and France intervened briefly at Archangel and Batum (138).

PLATE 12
The Russian Revolution

127 The tsar abdicated in March 1917. The 1909 stamps appeared imperforate, and the 1913 type surcharged on card for copper.

128 Kerensky's liberation design issued by the bolsheviks in November 1917.

129 1922 famine relief, unpriced because of inflation but sold at 20 + 5 roubles tax.

130 1922: imperial arms obliterated.

131 1923: the worker became the symbol of the Russian Socialist Federal Soviet Republic, which became part of the USSR in that year.

132 1932 factory girl: women had equality.

133 1957 new design of a miner

134 1942 war heroes: guerrillas in action

135 Azerbaijan Soviet Republic 1921, oilfield

Anti-Bolshevik Issues

136 Georgian National Republic 1919–21. The soviet republic joined Azerbaijan in the Transcaucasian Federation.

137 Ukraine, issue for Kharkov under white control in 1918

138 Foreign intervention: British occupation of Batum 1919–20, to protect oil interests.

PLATE 12

127

128

129

130

131

132

133

134

135

136

137

138

Peace brought the symbols of worker and peasant which have become characteristic of communist stamps (131–3). The 1923 rouble was worth a million paper roubles, but Lenin had saved the revolution and was able to reunite much of the old tsarist empire as the Union of Soviet Socialist Republics. There were thirteen of these, though the RSFSR outweighed the rest (131). 'White Russia' (Byelorussia) is one of these, and not a surviving tsarist regime. Five or six nations escaped bolshevik control, depending on the true freedom of Tuva in Mongolia, which issued attractive geometric stamps in the thirties, regarded by many collectors with some suspicion. Poland became independent for the first time since 1795, after a war led by the former Russian Marshal Piludski (184). The Finns seized their chance in 1917 led by another tsarist officer, Mannerheim (144). Partly because of their vigorous defence in three wars, they have preserved their freedom as the only former imperial territory still outside the soviet bloc; her Baltic neighbours Estonia (146), Latvia (142) and Lithuania (145), proved too vulnerable to survive the Nazi–Soviet Pact of 1939 (147). Poland took the ancient Lithuanian capital of Vilna and in return the free port of Memel was granted to Lithuania and renamed Klaipeda (143).

International recognition of these five states fitted Wilson's principle of national self-determination. The Versailles Peace Conference in 1919 had no difficulty over returning Alsace–Lorraine to France, and restoring Belgium. It was easy to punish the aggressor, Austria, by granting freedom to Hungary, nominally as a kingdom (150–1). Czechoslovakia emerged as a new, liberal state under the inspiration of Masaryk (188). Its large German population provoked Hitler's aggression. Serbia was enlarged greatly as the basis of the Kingdom of the Southern Slavs, Yugoslavia (156–7). Rumania doubled in size at Hungary's expense (152–3), which left the great city of Vienna with a tiny alpine republic which was given no chance to unite

with Germany (148–9). The industrial Saar was taken from Germany (162) and Danzig became a free port (141) which came under Nazi domination. The Rhineland was occupied until 1930 and demilitarised (173). Beside land ceded to the Poles and Czechs, Germany lost all her colonies overseas.

To preserve this new Europe, Wilson had instigated the League of Nations (12), though the USA Congress refused to become a member, despite modifications to the charter in 1920. This was intended to extend the work of the Hague Court (11), and valuable work was done by specialist agencies (13), but the withdrawal of Germany (which belonged only from 1926–33), Russia (a member from 1934–9), Brazil in 1926, Japan in 1933 and Italy in

PLATE 13
Self-Determination

139 Upper Silesia 1920–2, decided by a plebiscite to join Germany not Poland.
140 Fiume under the dictator-poet d'Annunzio 1919–21 was Italian 1924–46, then Yugoslav.
141 Danzig, a free port from 1919 to give Poland an outlet, Nazi controlled from 1933.
142 Latvia 1921–40 was under the pro-German dictator Ulmanis from 1934.
143 Memel 1920–3 captured by Lithuania, and subsequently part of Germany, then the USSR.
144 Finland declared independence in 1917, fought Russia in 1919–20, 1939–40 and 1941–4, under Marshal Mannerheim 1867–1948. He was head of state 1919–20 and 1944–6.
145 Lithuania 1918–40 lost Vilna to the Poles in 1919, was recognised 1922, and under the dictator Smetona from 1926. In 1940 it voted for incorporation into the USSR.
146 Estonia independent 1917–40, under the dictator Paets 1934–7, absorbed by Russia and occupied by Germany 1941–4.
147 Russian occupation of Latvia 1941. German army issues replaced these in November—Soviet stamps have been used since 1944.

PLATE 13

139

140

141

142

143

144

145

146

147

1937 meant that the most serious problems were not settled by debate. The League settled Upper Silesia (139), Danzig and the Saar, and established the effective system of mandates for Turkish and German territories (346, 368, 395, 398, 400, 404–6, 536).

Europe in 1920 thus contained far more nation states than it had in 1815. Three more adjustments followed. The poet d'Annunzio emulated Garibaldi by seizing the Adriatic port of Fiume (140). Yugoslavia had to give way until 1946; Albania, an autonomous province under a German prince, also came under Italian economic control (195). The Moslem Zog I became king in 1924 after a period of anarchy. The third new state was Ireland: thirty years of conflict led to a Home Rule Bill in 1912, which would have become law in 1914, but for the war. The Easter rising of 1916 and the post-war anarchy, increased Irish bitterness. A settlement from which the six protestant counties were excluded was reached in 1922 (158). Dominion status was granted (159), but a civil war followed. The Irish have free access to Britain, despite the post-war republican constitution (160), yet some in the south have never accepted the division (242).

By 1925 Europe seemed to be settled. Russia threatened world revolution, but was not strong enough to be a serious threat. After Lenin's death in 1924 (503), Stalin (216) became virtual dictator. He encouraged rapid industrial expansion, with an education system to feed this. Agriculture was drained to feed the factories, and massive purges took place. Some admired the new Russia, but more saw it as a threat to religion and security.

The youth of Europe set out to forget the war and enjoy the twenties. Modern art was excitingly free from naturalism (165) and a small income enabled many to join bohemian sets in London and Paris. Transport was fast and comfortable (166), even without flying. The motor car gave greater freedom still, though it took a terrible toll of life before

it was controlled by law (163). Morality also became less conventional, though tolerance did not extend to the throne in England (34). Europe was still the hub of the world, and France and Britain ruled over a great deal of it (33, 164). The neon-lit cities and new cinemas covered up persistent unemployment, however, and the main gestures towards the new era promised after the war were disarmament and the end of planning. Politics were not clear cut and both countries tried

PLATE 14
Central Europe

Austria
148 1919 symbol of the 'New Republic'
149 1934 definitive, to attract tourists

Hungary
150 'Republic' overprint 1918, followed by the 'harvesters' design inscribed only 'Magyar Posta', and in 1919 by the overprint 'Tanacs-Koztarsasig' for the Soviet Republic.
151 Admiral Horthy 1868–1957 overthrew Bela Kun 1919–20, and ruled as 'Regent' until 1944. He refused to crown Charles (96) in 1921, and was an unenthusiastic ally of Hitler.

Rumania
152 Ferdinand 1914–27, followed by Michael
153 Charles II returned to the throne and ran a fascist state 1930–40.
154 Michael 1927–30; deposed 1930–40. He was a communist king after 1945.

Bulgaria
155 Tsar Boris III 1918–43 fought Yugoslavia but not Russia, Simeon II survived only to 1946.

Yugoslavia
156 Alexander I 1921–34 united the Serbs, Croats and Slovenes in 1929. Portrait in 1931
157 Peter II 1934–45, at his accession. The Regent Paul was pro-German until the coup of 1941 which led to defiance and invasion (198).

PLATE 14

149

150

148

151

152

153

154

155

156

157

coalitions. The world slump of 1929 destroyed business confidence, and whole towns like Jarrow were destroyed. Rigid economy and the progress of fascism meant that the thirties were much more sober, but only Winston Churchill urged Britain to prepare for war (235). The late start did in fact give Britain a more modern air force by 1940, but it is a tragic irony that only munitions cured industrial poverty.

It has been an historical commonplace that World War II was the inevitable result of the Versailles Treaty. The new German Republic, with its capital at Weimar instead of Berlin, had to make enormous payments to the victors as well as losing territory and being disarmed. It made do with Bavarian stamps in its first year (168) and adopted the worker-image for its new designs (169). It was threatened by communists and monarchists. France occupied the Ruhr to squeeze money out faster in 1923; the Germans responded with passive resistance and printed money to feed the unemployed—hence the collapse of the mark (170–1). Stresemann became chancellor, and after making terms with France, issued a gold currency (172). The middle class was ruined, and seeds sown for Hitler's rise.

In 1925 the first Weimar head of state died (172); he was followed by a war hero, Hindenburg (174), a monarchist who had little influence on policy. The slump meant vast numbers of unemployed and skirmishes between communists and the national socialists who became the second largest party in 1930. In 1933 Hitler became chancellor, then Führer after Hindenburg's death, with the swastika as the twisted emblem of the Third Reich (175–6). Thus a new kind of one-party state was established, as carefully planned as Russia, but harnessing private industry. The return of the Saar was hailed as a victory (177). Mass support in rallies was channelled by military conscription, Hitler Youth (180) replaced boy scouts, and a modern air force was built.

PLATE 15
The Twenties and Thirties

Ireland
158 Provisional government for Ireland 1922
159 Irish Free State 1922
160 1937 new constitution as Eire, which became a republic in 1949.

161 Andorra, a tiny protectorate of France and Spain, issued stamps from 1928.
162 The Saar under French occupation 1920–34 returned to Germany by plebiscite (169).
163 Belgium: a victim of progress. The beautiful Queen Astrid killed on a motoring holiday in 1935.

France
164 Artistic centre of the world—the 1924 Exhibition of Modern Decorative Arts
165 International Colonial Exhibition 1931
166 The Atlantic: the maiden voyage of the *Normandie* in 1935, at the height of luxury liners' competitiveness.
167 Visit of George VI and Elizabeth to France 1938. Prophetic of the offer of common citizenship by Churchill in 1940

In 1936 the Olympic Games were staged in the fine new stadium in Berlin. Hitler sent his army into the Rhineland; the League of Nations, still occupied with its sanctions against Italy, only protested. Britain had made a naval agreement in 1935 which recognised the claim of Germany to be treated like other nations, and with the success of this limited aggression, Hitler was able to plan for his further advance. Nazi stamp design was very fine, reflecting the clean-cut architecture of the thirties by the Bauhaus school, though the founder, Gropius, was one of the increasing flow of refugees from the regime. German Jews had already started to settle in Palestine, but the rest of the world was slow to recognise the extent of Hitler's campaign, and after 1938 refugees could take no money with them.

PLATE 15

158

159

160

161

162

163

164

165

166

167

Between the occupation of the Rhineland and the rape of Austria, Europe's attention had been on Spain. Britain had survived the abdication crisis (34), and the new king (35–6) presided over an empire soberly facing the danger of war. In 1938 George VI and Queen Elizabeth visited France (167), but more crucial was the flight of his Prime Minister, Neville Chamberlain, to Munich. Hitler had swallowed Austria, and now claimed the 'return' of the former Austrian Sudetenland, where most of the inhabitants were German. He promised that this was his last claim, and Britain, France and Italy accepted this in September (189).

This advance was to give 'peace in our time', but it left the Czechs without much of their advanced industry, and with no clear frontier. The President, Eduard Benes, who had continued Masaryk's liberal tradition since 1935, felt obliged to resign. From 1941 he led the free Czechs in London (204) and resumed his office from 1945–8. He faced increasing pressure from Stalin, and resigned to allow a communist government. The rump of Czechoslovakia was forced to become a Nazi satellite in 1939 (190–1); nevertheless the Munich Agreement was well received at the time, and it is argued that it did give Britain and France more time to get ready for the terrifying prospect of aerial warfare on a massive scale. Gas masks and shelters were prepared, and evacuation plans drawn up for mothers and children.

When Britain and France did declare war in 1939, it was for a country which they could do nothing to help. Only Russia could have protected Poland. Ever since the civil war, Russia had been prepared for a possible war of defence. Stalin joined the League of Nations in 1934 after Germany had withdrawn, but Great Britain and France would not commit themselves to an anti-German treaty with him.

Russian stamps had lavishly portrayed the Soviet achievements, but they did not record the Molotov–Ribbentrop Pact of 23 August.

PLATE 16
The Weimar Republic and the Third Reich

168 1920: Bavarian stamps used up for economy
169 1921: workers on democratic definitives
170 1923: tenfold inflation by September
171 November reached 50,000,000,000 marks
172 December: Stresemann's new gold marks exchanged at a trillion to one.
173 The socialist President Ebert 1919–25. Overprint for the evacuation of the Rhineland
174 Mourning for the second president, Field-Marshal Hindenburg 1847–1934, who gave power to Hitler in 1933, hoping to control him.
175 Adolf Hitler 1889–1945 appeared first on definitive stamps in 1941.
176 The swastika appeared on air and official stamps in 1934.
177 1934: publicity for the Saar plebiscite (162)
178 1934: Nuremberg Nazi Party Congress
179 1936: the airship *Hindenburg*, which made prestige flights across the Atlantic.
180 1935: World Jamboree of Hitler Youth which replaced the Boy Scout movement.
181 1936 tenth anniversary of *Lufthansa* whose fast mailplanes were military prototypes.
182 1942 military fieldpost: the standard Ju 52 could not supply Stalingrad in 1942.

In return for non-aggression, Poland and the Baltic states were to be shared between the two great powers (147). Border incidents were arranged and the pincer blitz smashed the Polish forces who fought stubbornly against overwhelming odds; as in 1795, the state of Poland disappeared from the map (185). Although he had in effect been a dictator since 1926, the great Polish national leader, Piludski (who died in 1935) had seen the threat Hitler posed in 1933 and urged his ally France to act. In despair, he had made a non-aggression pact with Germany in 1934, which might well have warned Russia. Poland had no frontiers and little industry,

PLATE 16

168

169

170

171

172

173

174

175

176

177

178

179

180

181

182

although her pilots were among the best in the world (as the RAF was glad to discover), their army counterparts were still cavalry. In March 1939 Chamberlain despaired of the appeasement policy, and gave guarantees to Poland, Greece, Rumania and Turkey. On 3 September, Britain declared war on Germany and sent her forces to join the French but for eight months they did nothing but drop leaflets on German cities.

Before tracing the course of the war in Europe, Italy must be considered. There had been political street battles when the first war ended, and in 1919 Mussolini set up a Fascist Party to further social reform and national prestige (140). With the threat of civil war, Victor Emmanuel invited Mussolini to be prime minister in 1922. The latter adopted the title 'Duce', and in 1928–9 set up a one-party, one-constituency state. A set of definitives honoured ancient Rome as well as the king. This set was redrawn in 1945 without the axe and rods. A treaty with the pope (113) gave Europe a new city-state (194), and rallied catholic support to the new regime. Transport and industry were modernised quickly and before the invasion of Abyssinia in 1935 (393), there was a good deal of respect for Mussolini's work. The bombing and gassing of the only ancient, free African state provoked the verbal condemnation of the League of Nations, but no action beyond limited sanctions. As oil was not included, these achieved nothing. In 1936 Mussolini and Hitler set up the Axis. In 1939 Italy annexed Albania (195) and in June 1940 declared war on Britain and France. A Tripartite Pact brought Japan into the Axis, followed by Hungary, Rumania, Slovakia, Bulgaria and for a time, Yugoslavia (157).

In April 1940 Germany occupied Denmark (46) and Norway (196), and in May, the Netherlands. Holland and Belgium capitulated under the blitz and France, remembering the two earlier struggles, made peace under Pétain (199) in June. Part of France was left nominally free under the puppet government

PLATE 17
Munich

Poland
183 1921: symbol of peace with Russia
184 Marshal Piludski 1867–1935. Head of state 1919–21, commander to 1923 and after a coup d'etat in 1926, virtually dictator. The stamp commemorates the Polish legion of 1914.
185 1939–45 Nazi Occupation

Czechoslovakia
186 1934: twentieth anniversary of Czech legions in World War I—enrolment in France
187 1919: the young republic welcomes the legion home. It controlled the trans-Siberian railway 1918–20 and was the strongest army in Russia, but was never aggressively anti-bolshevik.
188 Tomas Masaryk 1850–1937, invented the state of Czechoslovakia in exile during the war. As a liberal and a scholar he had great influence in the peace. President 1918–35
189 After the Munich Agreement in September 1938 the Sudetenland was ceded to Germany—1942 issue for Bohemia and Moravia.
190 The rump was defenceless and came under German protection as Slovakia in 1939.
191 Dr Josef Tiso, the Nazi puppet ruler

at Vichy but the whole of mainland Europe, apart from Sweden and Switzerland, was organised to further the Nazi war effort (197).

British stamps of the time gave no hint of the danger after the Dunkirk evacuation. The centenary of the first stamps was marked, and in 1941 paler colours were used for economy. Apart from the victory issue, the set to mark the liberation of the Channel Islands (210) is the only hint of the closeness of the Nazis in 1940, though a fine 'Battle of Britain' series appeared in 1965. The British post office now issues regular commemoratives, and it is possible to build up a retrospective history. These cover a wide range of anniversaries and are outside the scope of this book.

PLATE 17

183

184

185

186

187

188

189

190

191

Hitler gave up hope of invasion and set out to blockade Britain and bomb her cities by night. British stamp collectors were not without propaganda issues, however, as those colonies which supported de Gaulle issued sets with the Cross of Lorraine after 1942, and the following year the free Norwegian, Polish and Dutch governments did the same (201–4). The sale of these helped the war effort and the stamps were put into use in 1945, unlike the widely sold 'Abyssinian Red Cross' stamps. The packet warned: 'These stamps will never be catalogued', and schoolchildren bought them as a rarity! They were used with a 'V' overprint in 1945. The author remembers the fearful pride the first Hitler stamps brought to children. The stamps of this era are undervalued, partly as many were remaindered.

In 1941 the Germans turned east and made rapid inroads into Russia (200), Yugoslavia (198) and Greece. The British were driven from Crete, but Malta resisted successfully and was awarded a collective medal (235). Some Croats and Russians welcomed the Nazis, but their treatment of the Slavs provoked partisan warfare in Serbia under Tito (234) and united the Russian people, led by their clergy. Stalin became the 'Father' of his people. The battles of Stalingrad and Alamein in 1942, followed by the occupation of French North Africa (206), were the turning points of the war. British stamps were overprinted 'EAF' and 'MEF' in 1942 for use in the occupied Italian colonies. They were re-issued with their names overprinted in 1948.

In 1943 the allies invaded Sicily and Italy (207). Stalin, Roosevelt and Churchill (299), had their first meeting at Teheran, extending the close relations of the Atlantic Charter. Mussolini was overthrown, Italy changed sides, but the Germans rescued the Duce and set up a Repubblica Sociale Italiana which issued two series. The conquest of the peninsula was slow, though Rome was saved. In 1944 Normandy was invaded and the Germans were steadily

PLATE 18
The Spread of Fascism

192 Fasces appeared on the royal portrait in 1929 and propaganda labels were added in 1942.
193 1941: Hitler and Mussolini appeared on Italian and Italian East African issues.
194 Mussolini's Lateran Treaty in 1929 ended the sixty-year isolation of the Vatican city. The Vatican became a tiny independent state.
195 Greece successfully resisted the Italian invasion in 1940 and occupied Albania prior to the German attack.
196 Vidkun Quisling 1887–1945, Nazi party leader, traitor and puppet ruler of Norway
197 Dutch charity stamp 1942 in support of the small enlistment in the Axis forces
198 Anton Pavelitch, ruler of the puppet state in Croatia 1941–5
199 Marshal Pétain 1856–1951, war hero who surrendered to Germany in 1940 and ran part of France from Vichy until the liberation of 1944.
200 Hitler invaded Russia in 1941.

driven back by overwhelming force on both fronts (205, 207–9). The Fourth French Republic was declared by de Gaulle (236).

The allies confirmed their policy for the unconditional surrender of Germany and Japan at Yalta in 1944, and arranged for the division of Europe at Potsdam in 1945. The Germans fought bitterly until the Russians reached Berlin (211), and Hitler committed suicide. The European war seemed to be over but conflict over the peace had already begun and the German problem is still not finally resolved. Churchill had wanted to invade Yugoslavia, where he had supported the coup of 1941 and aided royalist and communist partisans; however, it was agreed that Russia should occupy the east. Germany was to be divided into zones, including a French area taken from the Anglo–American zone (218), and Austria and Berlin were to be under four-power control.

PLATE 18

192

193

194

195

196

197

198

199

200

A peace treaty was made with Austria in 1955, when it joined Sweden, Switzerland and Finland as a neutral state. Its stamps have been costumes, views and commemoratives as in the thirties. Germany proved more complex, however, as their treatment of occupied areas had been barbaric. The Nuremburg trials of Nazis are unique in law, but were regarded as vital. In 1945–6 the German civilian population was starving, while Russia was removing corn from Prussian farms for her own needs, and taking complete factories as reparations. Britain and America pooled resources but grew suspicious of Russian motives. The exiled London Poles were never given equal status by the communist government of Lublin. The Polish secret army had not been helped in the Warsaw Rising of 1944. In 1948 Russia closed the road to Berlin, the city was now partitioned (214), and the allies supplied it by air. Thereafter the western mark became several times more valuable (214, 220) than the eastern, and refugees flowed into West Germany. Ten years later Russia demanded an end to military occupation, and in 1961 the East German government built the Wall to seal off the west. Chancellor Brandt's initiative brought an understanding between the two Germanies but not until 1972.

By 1948 the Cold War was a reality and the 'Iron Curtain' dropped along the Elbe. Many Poles and their neighbours settled in the west; the British Museum has a superb collection of stamps and postmarks donated by Mr M. A. Bojanowicz which shows in detail the military and post-war history of the Polish exiles. Czechoslovakia was the last state to become communist—with the exception of the independent policies of Tito (234) and Albania's defection to China in 1961, the power blocs have not changed. Two rival republics were set up in Germany (216–7, 222–4). American and Russian forces still face each other there and the two states have reflected the influence of their protectors.

PLATE 19
Free Europe and Victory

Propaganda stamps issued in London for forces fighting with the allies.
201 Norway 1943, the destroyer *Sleipner*
202 Netherlands 1944, cruiser *De Ruyter*
203 Poland 1943: coastal command Wellington. The only issue not sold after liberation.
204 Czechoslovakia 1945: Staff-Captain Vasatko, hero of the Battle of Britain
205 Moscow portrait of Masaryk for the liberation of western Slovakia 1945
206 The allies occupied Vichy North Africa in 1942: de Gaulle's Free French symbol, the Cross of Lorraine, on the 1944 definitive.
207 1943 issue for occupied Sicily
208 1944: liberation of Belgium
209 1945: liberation of Alsase–Lorraine
210 1948: third anniversary of liberation of the Channel Islands, the only part of Great Britain occupied, and the first regional stamp.

It is now a quarter of a century since the breach of 1948, and there is little chance of a third European war. Tension is now in the 'third world' of former colonies. There have been enormous changes in Europe which are not so easily discerned from stamps as they have involved political evolution and not violent change. West and east united in the military alliances of NATO (268), and the Warsaw Pact respectively. The GFR reintroduced conscription in 1956, but Britain abolished it and France left NATO without apparent danger. The west now relies on a nuclear umbrella, which could cause such devastation that there would be nothing left for the victor. Indeed since the Cuban crisis (306) the two rival powers have come to a limited understanding and both are concerned with China. The communist party is important in France and Italy but now works democratically in the west.

National risings in Hungary in 1956 under Imre Nagy, and Czechoslovakia in 1968 under Dubcek, were put down by the Red Army,

PLATE 19

201

202

203

204

205

206

207

208

209

210

but there have been no purges comparable to Stalin's since Khruschev became the soviet leader in 1953. He lost his power in 1964, but was allowed to retire in peace. The improved standard of living and cultural contact with the west has led to criticism within the USSR, but justified national pride in economic and technological achievements (228–9) has removed a lot of the Soviet fear of the west. Agriculture still has not recovered from Stalin's purges, and Russia now imports American grain and trades freely in the west. There are diplomatic relations with the pope, and communist Poland remains Catholic.

The whole of Europe was impoverished by the war. An Organisation for European Economic Co-operation was set up to deal with the generous USA aid (238, 271). Idealism and rationing combined to extend social care after Scandinavia had paved the way. Coalition and Labour Governments in Britain, and the new Christian Democrat parties in Europe laid the foundations for just and healthy societies. Churchill had seen the need for European unity in 1940: he made a further challenge in Zurich in 1946 (167, 235).

'We must build a kind of United States of Europe. In this way only will hundreds of millions of toilers be able to regain the simple joys and hopes which make life worth living.'

In 1950 Robert Schuman proposed the merging of Europe's coal and steel industries. This was a logical extension of Benelux and OEEC (238), Great Britain would not participate. Six countries did, and seven years later moved to full economic unity (239). Massive, modern industries were developed which, by the sixties, were superior to the British. The standard of living in the EEC passed the British, as may be seen from the steady decline in the value of the pound.

Britain gave independence to her empire after the war, beginning with India in 1948 (445). This was done largely by consent. She has retained responsibility for several small territories, which marked the royal Silver Wedding in 1972 (37). This set may be compared with

PLATE 20
The Division of Germany

211 Russian occupation of Berlin 1945
212 General issue for Saxony 1945–6
213 Relief fund, Leipzig 1946
214 1947–8 issue of the civil government, overprinted for the soviet zone after the Berlin confrontation in 1948.
215 1946: reconstruction of Dresden, victim of the most massive bombing on record
216 German Democratic Republic: the first anniversary of the death of Stalin 1954
217 Walter Ulbricht, 1893–1973, the organiser and ruler of the GDR, and the closest disciple of Stalin
218 French zone 1945–6, followed by issues for Baden, Rhineland, Palatinate, Saar and Württemberg
219 Anglo–American zone military government 1945
220 1948 issue in the reformed currency
221 West Berlin has been a political unit since 1948. One boundary is the Brandenburg Gate, shown on this 1949 stamp.
222 Definitive design for the Federal Republic, 1951
223 President Heuss 1949–59
224 President Heinemann 1969

the Jubilee issue of 1935 and the Coronation of 1953 to see the reduction in crown control. The British Commonwealth has continued, but the withdrawal of the two white regimes in South Africa and the closer ties of the old dominions with the USA, has left this a very loose association. The prosperity of the fifties brought large-scale immigration to England, which is now controlled, and East African nationalism has created a new wave of British Asians. The formation of EFTA in 1959 was intended to rival the EEC, but from 1961 it was clear that the Common Market (which was finally enlarged in January 1973 (243)) was more effective. Labour and Conservative Governments have followed similar policies since the war. The post office has acknow-

PLATE 20

211

212

213

214

215

216

217

218

219

220

221

222

223

224

ledged demands for regional autonomy and increased its revenue by the issue of stamps for Scotland, Northern Ireland, Wales, the Isle of Man, Guernsey and Jersey (242). The three islands now have their own postal administrations. Ulster was given a new con-constitution in 1973 to allow further Catholic participation in government.

The Fourth Republic in France recovered slowly from the war. National honour seemed to demand the maintenance of the empire, and disastrous wars were fought in Indo-China and Algeria (384, 465). There were frequent changes of government, foreseen by de Gaulle in 1946 when he retired from political life, but a powerful civil service built up the economy. Great Britain and France tried to overthrow Nasser in Egypt in 1956, but the USA quickly stopped this last military initiative. In 1958 the French army revolted in Algeria, and de Gaulle was recalled. He set up a Fifth Republic with a strong president, and his party has continued to form the French government. There was some fear of a military dictatorship in 1958, but the General made a settlement in Algeria and then restored the international standing of France by treaties with Chancellor Adenauer in Germany and with Russia. He insisted on a separate nuclear strike force, but opened relations with China. He acted throughout with massive support from the French people, and showed that a charismatic leadership can be practised within democracy. He was followed by President Pompidou in 1969, who continued his policies until 1974.

Europe in the seventies has moved a long way towards the USA standard of living. Many problems accompany this prosperity which depends on ample cheap raw materials from poorer countries, and there has been a growing sense of responsibility towards the underdeveloped regions. The United Nations has helped, but genuine European cooperation is only just beginning, and there is little prospect of political union. Materialism has come to dominate east and west Europe.

PLATE 21
The Iron Curtain

225 Rumania changed to support the Russians in 1944, though the king did not abdicate until 1947 (154). The 1955 series is typical of communist pictures of workers. The schoolboy is, in this case, a symbol of progress.

226 Poland lost a tenth of its population during the war and Warsaw, as shown on this 1945 issue, was devastated in the 1944 rising.

227 Hungary officially became a republic in 1946. The definitive issues are in units of thousand pengos at the beginning of an inflation that rose to 500,000 billions.

228 USSR: the Twenty-second Party Congress of 1961: the stamps issued in 1962, in the middle of the 1958–65 Seven-Year Plan, point to the fulfilment of Khruscev's claim to overtake the USA by 1980.

229 The Soviet Union put the first man into space in 1961. This shows the Mars I space station in 1964.

230 Bulgaria celebrated the twenty-fifth anniversary of 'liberation' in 1969.

231 Czechoslovakia: 1969 fiftieth anniversary of the Slovak Republican Council

232 Yugoslavia was liberated by communist partisans with British help. This partisan commemoration design of 1945 was overprinted in 1949 for the revised title Federal People's Republic.

233 1947: Yugoslav military government of Venezia, Guilia and Istria, which apart from Trieste, were incorporated in that year. Trieste was shared with Italy in 1954.

234 1967 Marshal Tito's seventy-fifth birthday. The only communist leader to maintain policies independent of Moscow and Peking.

It has helped to remove the danger of renewed nationalist wars, but it has not brought satisfaction. France and Britain have experienced massive industrial unrest, there have been strikes in Poland. Education has become the method of social progress, but has proved no more successful than religion in promoting wisdom.

PLATE 21

225

226

227

228

229

230

231

232

233

234

PLATE 22
Europa

235 Malta, now independent and demanding high rents for bases, joined the western world in mourning Winston Churchill 1874–1966. The George Cross appears on his left.

236 France commemorated Charles de Gaulle 1890–1970 in 1971. He led the free French from 1940, but withdrew from politics from 1946 to 1958. He set up the Fifth Republic with its powerful elected presidency.

237 Greece was a republic 1924–35 and was occupied by Germany 1941–4. A communist revolt was overcome with British help. A new threat in 1967 led to a right-wing army coup which exiled Constantine, king since 1964. The 1956 stamp shows him as crown prince aged sixteen.

238 The liberated Low Countries formed an economic union after liberation. A fuller union of sixteen, the OEEC, was formed in 1947 to administer Marshall Aid. The Netherlands marked the twenty-fifth anniversary in 1969.

239 The Treaty of Rome in 1957 brought in the European Economic Community of France, Germany, Italy and the Benelux countries.

240 Since 1956 annual designs have marked European postal co-operation, usually with identical symbols on every stamp: the 1958 symbol on the French issue.

241 In 1959 Britain, Scandinavia, Austria, Switzerland and Portugal formed a Free Trade Association, marked by Denmark in 1967.

242 Northern Ireland: 1958. In contrast to the growth of larger units, there has been an upsurge of nationalism in Europe, and some separatist MPs have been elected. The problem of Ulster, left from 1922, is still unresolved.

243 Britain and others, applied to enter 1961–3 and 1967–9. The resignation of de Gaulle made enlargement possible and Britain, Denmark and Ireland joined in 1973.

PLATE 22

235

236

237

238

239

241

240

242

243

CHAPTER THREE
THE AMERICAN CONTINENT

America is divided into three clearly defined sections. The north consists of former British colonies, and though this was originally the less-desirable region, it is today the richest and most advanced in the world. The south consists of former Spanish and Portuguese territories, while the West Indians are of African stock. The indigenous population survives in reservations, or the Amazon jungle. By the time the first stamps appeared in the USA in 1847, most of the states on the mainland were free; their struggles were recent and their heroes have become national symbols. The democratic fear of tyranny led to the convention that living people were not portrayed on stamps. Most Latin-American states have followed this, and in this chapter it has been necessary to use retrospective issues. Some examples which commemorate the discoverers and colonists are included, as the whole history of America falls within the modern period—these regular issues would make a fascinating small collection.

By 1847 the United States was established as a major power. It had fought a naval war with England in 1812, and the Monroe Doctrine of 1823 (249) warned European powers against interference in the newly independent states in the south and laid the foundation of an isolationist foreign policy which lasted until 1917. From then the USA rapidly became the most powerful nation in the world.

Before this the USA had to face its great internal conflict. Slavery, which had been abolished in the British colonies in 1833, was the great moral issue. This was only one factor in the growing breach between the old

colonial, aristocratic south, and the north. The new population came from all over Europe to develop industry and the huge, mechanised prairie farms. Abraham Lincoln (251), born on a small freehold, was fighting

PLATE 23
The Formation of the Union

244 The 400th anniversary of the discovery of America was marked by a long series in 1893.

245–6 The colonial development, illustrated by the tercentenary of Nicolet's landing at Wisconsin in 1634, and the Pilgrim Fathers in 1620.

247 George Washington 1732–99 and Benjamin Franklin 1706–90 (256) have appeared on every USA definitive series since 1847. Franklin drafted the constitution of 1787; Washington was president 1789–97. 1932: this is the first of twelve portraits commemorating his birth.

248–50 Three more examples of the regular issues which mark the colonisation, expansion and establishing of states within the USA. The Louisiana purchase stamps include the portrait of James Monroe, president 1817–25, who issued the famous warning against European intervention in the Americas.

251 Abraham Lincoln, president 1861–5, fought the Civil War to preserve the Union and abolish slavery—the stamp from the 1938 series.

252 The first of five annual issues from 1961 marking the battles of the Civil War.

253 Confederate states: Jefferson Davis elected president of the south 1862–5. He was imprisoned 1865–6 and died 1889.

PLATE 23

244

245

246

247

248

249

250

251

252

253

to preserve the national unity; the death of the brilliant frontier lawyer in 1865 gave the USA the first of its martyrs by political assassination. His opponent, Jefferson Davis (253), was fighting to keep a way of life which machines would make uneconomic. The race problem in the USA today stems from the poor conditions forced on the negro in the north.

The war did not solve the social and economic rift, but the opening up of the west first for herding and then for agriculture (255), provided a new outlet. Lawlessness was a problem, and a second president died in 1881 (254). Five million immigrants entered the USA, and a host of sub-cultures grew up. The constitution granted total religious liberty, Christianity flourished in myriad forms but all reflected the original New England sense of destiny and social conscience.

War with Spain in 1898 was seen as a crusade against colonialism. It was provoked by the sinking of the *Maine* at Havana, though Spain did not want to fight. The USA absorbed Puerto Rico (117), and took the Philippines as colonies (515). Independent Hawaii was also annexed as an outer defence and ceased to issue its own stamps (514). Thus the USA became a colonial power, and the stage was set for the rivalry with Japan in the thirties. Cuba, the largest of the West Indies, was occupied by USA forces (256), although independence was granted in 1902, the USA retained special powers until 1935. In 1904 the USA leased land from Panama to build the canal (295)—the Nicaraguan stamp showing a volcano helped to settle the site. Spain had completely lost its role in the Americas.

Relations with Britain at the height of her power were mixed. Marriages became common between the 'cousins' (34), including the parents of Churchill (235). On the other hand, the Irish population was very hostile towards England, and there was a strong German community. The aggressive Republican, 'Teddy' Roosevelt, president 1901–9, hero of the Cuban war and initiator of the canal, was

pro-British. He was defeated by Woodrow Wilson in 1912 (257). In 1916 Wilson won again as a pacifist, but the unrestricted U-boat war, and a plot to bring Mexico into the hostilities, made the USA declare war in

PLATE 24
The Growth of United States Power

254 James Garfield appeared on a new 5c in 1882 to commemorate his brief presidency and assassination in 1881.

255 A contemporary photograph of farming in the west, on the Trans-Mississippi Exposition series of 1898

256 Spanish–American War 1898. Stamps of the 1894 series were overprinted and surcharged for use in conquered Cuba: Benjamin Franklin (247).

257 Woodrow Wilson, president 1912–21, brought the USA into World War I in 1917, and inspired the establishment of the League of Nations. A new 17c value followed his death in 1924 as a memorial portrait.

258 Warren Harding, president 1921–3, who died in office. This portrait appeared first as a memorial, then in 1925 as a 1½c definitive.

259 Henry Ford 1863–1947, the inventor of mass production. Prominent Americans series 1965

260 1933 issue marking the Antarctic flight of Rear-Admiral Byrd, who flew over the North Pole in 1926, the Atlantic 1927 and the South Pole in 1929. He made further expeditions 1933- 46, and died in 1957.

261 The dedication of the Boulder Dam 1935 was part of Roosevelt's first New Deal 1933–5.

262 Symbol of west-coast prosperity: the San Francisco Exhibition of 1939

263 The 'China Clipper' design of 1935 was reissued for the regular Pacific airmail in 1937. The USA was already setting the trend of civil aviation.

264 Independence Day slogan stamp for 1942

265 Roosevelt's famous four freedoms in 1943, arose from the Atlantic Charter of 1941.

PLATE 24

254

255

256

257

258

259

260

261

262

263

264

265

1917—Wilson guided the peace conference. Harding, President 1921–3, opposed membership of the League, and the USA did not join.

The USA was isolated politically. Its energy was used in building up the motor, cinema and aviation industries (259, 263, 266), Charles Lindbergh flew the Atlantic solo in 1927, Byrd made a series of flights from 1926, and the USA was quickly covered by a network of airlines (260). The Pacific airmail started in 1935, and the Atlantic in 1939 (263). These showed that isolation could not continue.

The thirties were soured by the Wall Street slump of 1929, and by rural depression. In 1932 F. D. Roosevelt was elected (267), with his 'New Deal' (261). His programme of public works restored the economy; he formed ties with England and France, recognised the USSR and won a massive election victory in 1936. Before Pearl Harbour he had provided armaments for Britain, and helped to protect convoys. National defence stamps in 1940 marked the start of General Marshall's rapid mobilisation (271) and stamps of 1942–3 made clear to the American people what they were fighting for (264–5). The war had no direct impact on the homeland, but films recorded the struggles of the marines in the Pacific and post-war stamps honoured the forces (266).

Roosevelt died at the moment of triumph. Since his time, the story of the USA has been world history, though mainly concerned with Europe and Asia (268–70). Truman, president 1945–53, did not trust Stalin, and fought in Korea to contain communism—the USA had close ties with Chiang Kai-shek and refused to recognise the communist government 1948–72. John F. Kennedy (274) reasserted the Monroe principle in the tense situation after the USSR began to arm Cuba with nuclear weapons.

The USA maintained its lead in nuclear potential (269) but was shocked when the USSR took the lead in space flight (229). This led to the space race, which the USA won with its moon landing in 1969 (275). This, and the war in Vietnam, have proved very costly, and there is retrenchment and a hint of isolation under President Nixon. The United Nations, which fought the Korean war, is now more likely to criticise USA policies (16–17).

The unpopularity of the Vietnam war came as a shock to many Americans, who saw it as a continuing crusade for freedom. So too did the realisation that poverty and discontent were rife below post-war affluence. Kennedy's election was a liberal triumph, and Lyndon Johnson 1963–9 carried out a programme of social care—the new concern is shown in recent stamps. USA stamps used to show

PLATE 25
The United States as a World Power

266 1944: the fiftieth anniversary of the film industry also honouring the troops who were fighting on the Pacific islands.
267 Franklin D. Roosevelt, president 1934–45, with the White House on the memorial set
268 1952: the third anniversary of NATO, for rearming Europe against communism.
269 1955: an international movement to harness nuclear energy for peaceful use.
270 1960 conference of SEATO, the alliance formed in 1954 for protection against China.
271 General Marshall 1880–1959 who built up the first mass USA army, and then planned the reconstruction of Europe after the war. He won the Nobel Peace Prize in 1953.
272 Dwight D. Eisenhower 1890–1969, supreme commander in Europe 1943–5 and 1950–2, and Republican president 1953–61
273 John Foster Dulles who, as foreign secretary 1953–9, maintained a firm policy against communism. Memorial stamp of 1960
274 John F. Kennedy, 1917–63, president from 1961, was assassinated in his prime.
275 USA moon landing 1969. Neil Armstrong is the first living American to appear on a stamp.
276 In contrast, this 1969 issue pinpoints the problem of urban sprawl and pollution.

PLATE 25

266

267

268

269

270

271

272

273

274

275

276

national parks and wildlife, but they now remind the public of drug abuse, the need for family planning, and social care. Special series in 1970–1 advocated the control of pollution in cities and the preservation of historical monuments (276). The USA can still supply wheat to Russia and India; though her surplus is less, she will continue to be vital in issues of world security.

In the far north of America were small colonies which remained loyal to England. In 1784 the United Empire Loyalists joined them and gave the north an ethos. Quebec had been French, and had no affinity with the New England states. The Earl of Durham put down a rebellion in 1839, and though recalled, his report laid the basis of colonial government. The provinces (277–9) wrangled, but diplomacy led to the British North America Act 1867, which established the first dominion, a self-governing territory under the crown (281).

The purchase of Alaska from Russia in the same year gave the USA an interest in the north. The Klondyke gold rush of 1896 led to co-operation, and Canadian development has reflected that of the USA. Loyalty to Britain has been strong, however, and forces went to Europe in both world wars (84–5, 284). The Statute of Westminster in 1931 made clear dominion autonomy, while the Ottawa Conference in 1932 established imperial preferences, and protected Canadian wheat prices.

Since 1946 Canada has been a member of NATO and been a leading member of the new British commonwealth (285–6). She has also shown concern for world problems (287) and taken a part in peace-keeping missions for the United Nations. Potentially wealthy in proportion to population, the major political issue has been a movement to separate the French-speaking province of Quebec. This is akin to regional nationalism in Britain and some other parts of Europe.

The Spanish colonies in southern America were inspired by the Americans and French

to overthrow their rulers. Spain was a client of Britain and France after 1815, and could not manage a series of wars against the will of the USA (256) and the British fleet. A series of romantic soldiers fought to free the mainland (288–90) with the help of the English Admiral Cochrane, who served in turn Chile, Brazil and Greece. Cuba and Puerto Rico, with their West Indian economies, remained loyal (117).

Brazil's emancipation from Portugal was different. The court moved to Rio de Janiero in 1808 to escape from Napoleon, it was sent back to Lisbon in 1821 and the king's son Pedro became emperor of independent Brazil. He abdicated in 1831, but his son (291) ruled until 1889. The new monarchy made progress and slavery was abolished in 1888. The army

PLATE 26
British North America

277 New Brunswick 1860
278 Nova Scotia 1860
279 Colony of Canada 1859 inscribed in sterling and dollar currency.
280 Newfoundland 1911, Coronation of George V and Queen Mary (33). The island joined the Dominion of Canada in 1949.

Dominion of Canada
281 1897 Diamond Jubilee of Queen Victoria
282 1898: the establishment of imperial penny postage in the heyday of the empire. Inland rates for surface mail still apply for mail within the British commonwealth.
283 1939 the queen and Princess Margaret on the issue for the visit of the royal family
284 War effort 1942: large numbers of RAF pilots were trained in Canada during the war.
285 1959: tenth anniversary of NATO (268)
286 Commonwealth Parliamentary Association Conference, Ottawa 1966
287 The Colombo Plan of 1950 was for the rich nations to help Asian development. This issue of 1961 marked the beginning of the UN Development Decade.

PLATE 26

277

278

279

280

281

282

283

284

285

286

287

copied the USA with a federal constitution in 1891, but the country stayed mostly feudal until the fascist-style regime of Getuilo Vargas 1930–45. Brazil's wealth depended on the export of coffee and rubber, and the rapid population growth kept it the largest state in the south (303)—it fought Germany from 1942. A new capital, Brasilia, has been built.

The Spanish La Plata was divided into the Argentine, Paraguay, Bolivia and a small Uruguay as a buffer to Brazil. Chile and Peru continued in the west, while New Granada was split into Ecuador, Colombia, Venezuela and a union of Salvador, Costa Rica, Honduras, Nicaragua and Guatemala. Bolivar's dream of a united state was vain, though his name was given to a split from Peru. The central states split in 1838 and rapidly realised the value of stamps as exports —they indicated their membership of the UPU, and the date, for many years (10, 296). There were regular wars between the powers (293) but the famous statue, Christ of the Andes, records one occasion when the wiser counsels prevailed. It was erected in 1904, appearing on an Argentine stamp in 1934.

The largest and most volatile of the central states was Mexico. It was a monarchy 1822–3 and 1863–7. It lost Texas, New Mexico and California to the USA in the war of 1846–8. Political anarchy held sway 1911–16 (294) and a radical regime followed: Calles ruled 1924–35 and persecuted the church. His relations with the USA were shattered by the nationalisation of oil in 1938 and there was no improvement until 1947, since which time Mexico has recorded steady progress on long sets of stamps, including the 1968 Olympics (305).

There are similarities and contrasts between South and North America. The railways did a certain amount to open up the hinterland, but the Panama Canal (295) and air travel were more important. A German company, SCADTA, began to operate in 1919, and in 1932 St Exupéry's powerful novel *Night Flight* described the danger faced by pioneers (292,

PLATE 27
Latin America to 1945

The liberators have been symbols to the South American republics, like Washington in the USA.

288 Simon Bolivar 1783–1850, fought for the independence of Colombia, Venezuela, Ecuador, Peru and Bolivia 1812–25, but he failed to establish a federation: Venezuela stamp 1893.

289 José de San Martin 1778–1856, fought in the Argentine 1812, Chile 1818 and Peru until 1821. He favoured a united monarchy: 1959 stamp.

290 Bernado O'Higgins 1778–1842, fought to free Chile 1812–18, then ruled as dictator to 1823: Chilean stamp 1911.

Brazil, the former Portuguese colony

291 Pedro II 1826–94, emperor 1831–89, was a liberal scholar, but the army replaced him by a federal republic: portrait of 1866.

292 A biplane on an archaic design in 1920

Peru fought Chile unsuccessfully 1879–83

293 Morales Bermudez 1894, one of a series of military dictators after the Chilean and civil wars. Peace came under Pierola in 1895.

Mexico, an empire under the French protégé Maximillian 1863–7, then a dictatorship

294 Revoluntary provisional for Sonora 1914: initials of Gobernio Contitucionalista

Canal Zone, leased from Panama by the USA.

295 General G. W. Goethals built the canal. 1903–14, after de Lesseps' failure in 1889. Portrait issue 1934: Goethals died in 1928.

296 Guatemala 1932 and 1942. The design combines early art with a slogan for coffee.

297 Paraguay fought Bolivia in the Chaco war 1932–5. Commemorative issue 1957

298 Chile: one of the elegant air set 1934

299 Colombia celebrated peace in 1945 with the heads of Stalin, Roosevelt and Churchill.

PLATE 27

288

289

290

291

292

293

294

295

296

297

298

299

298). The south had depended on the exports of primary products until World War II, however, and land was owned by the rich. The Indians had been dispossessed long before, the European part of the population lacked new blood and lived the luxurious life of the nineteenth century.

Massive foreign investment made the south prosperous in the twenties, but the slump cut trade and led to another period of political instability. As in Europe, dictatorship was the only cure—Venezuela was ruled by Gomez from 1908–35, Chile by Allesandri 1932–8 and Cuba by Batista 1933–59. One of the most pointless struggles was the Chaco war 1932–5 (297). Salamanca became president of Bolivia in 1931 and rejected League of Nations help, and decided to conquer the disputed desert. The victory of Paraguay was helped by shortages of water, and both sides were impoverished.

Trade had begun to recover by the late thirties, the battle of the Atlantic was a further stimulus to local industries, the population grew rapidly and more lived in the cities. Despite the regular revolutions, Bolivia had sixty in a hundred years, little was done to distribute wealth. The rich sympathised with the Axis, and the left were hostile to the USA. The Argentine remained neutral during the war, and six other states did not join with the united nations until 1945: most celebrated the victory (299).

The Argentine moved closest to a modern state under Colonel Juan Peron. He built up his authority from 1943, and was elected to the presidency in 1946 and 1951. He was ably supported by his charming and devout wife, Eva, who organised trade unions and women's movements (301). His five-year plans were more propaganda than sound economics, and with the trade recession following the end of the Korean war and the continuing opposition of the church, he fell in 1955 (302). In 1957 control was less, but the Peronist Party continued. In 1972 he returned from exile in Spain, and was again elected president in 1973.

Since the war, Latin America has been part of the developing world. It faces great problems of health and education (302–3). The combination of Asian population growth with American expectations has produced its own form of revolution. In 1956 Fidel Castro landed in Cuba with a tiny force, built up an army of peasants, and in 1959 expelled Batista. Two years later he declared himself a communist, and the installation of Russian missiles in 1962 was the gravest threat to world peace since 1948. Soviet economic aid has kept Cuba solvent, despite USA opposition. Castro's communism is more Chinese than Russian.

PLATE 28
Latin America since 1945

Argentine was under the popular President Juan Peron who ruled 1946–55.
300 The end of the Five-Year Plan 1951
301 Eva Peron appeared on the definitive issue after her death in 1952.

302 Dominican Republic was ruled by Rafael Trujillo 1930–61. It was host to the Pan-American Health Conference in 1950.
303 Brazil held a National Education Week in 1963. Illiteracy is a grave problem.
304 Chile 1969, like Canada and others, marked Expo 70 in Osaka, recognising Japan's enormous importance in modern world trade.
305 Mexico, host to the 1968 Olympic Games, issued five special series (21–8).
306 Cuba has been ruled by Fidel Castro since the 1959 revolution. Its stamps reflect East-European design: museum issue 1965.

Revolution has not succeeded anywhere else on the continent: Castro's colleague, Che Guevara, was killed in Bolivia in 1967 and has become a cult-hero to young radicals throughout the world. In 1965 USA marines, supported by the Organisation of American States, put down a rising in nearby San Domingo (302). There are economic institutions similar to Europe, CACOM and

PLATE 28

300

301

302

303

304

305

306

LAFTA, and in the West Indies CARIFTA, but the problem of poverty is much greater.

In 1972 Chile elected a Marxist, Allende, as president. He declared that he would bring about reform by constitutional means, but he faced enormous opposition from the middle class and revolution followed in 1973. The old systems are far from dead, but nationalism will become rarer though Salvador and Honduras were involved in a minor war in 1969.

The Spanish were not as concerned with race as the English and French, and there is a large creole population in the republics. Apart from Cuba, the West Indian islands are remarkable in that the population is mainly African, taken there against their consent. Until the expansion of tourism, made possible by air travel, Europeans regarded life in the sun as an uncomfortable way of earning money, and immigration was never encouraged (320).

The islands were first important as a landfall on the way to the Eldorado of the Spanish silver mines. It was realised that sugar and tropical fruits were more valuable than metal, and the old privateer bases became trading and naval ports. Other assets were discovered, like the asphalt lake on Trinidad. Some of them were too small for anything but subsistence farming and fishing.

Haiti was the first independent West Indian state; it threw off French rule in 1804 and was ruled by a former slave, the Emperor Jacques Delines until 1806. It has had a series of charismatic dictators, who have encouraged primitive African religion. The Duvalier family has ruled since 1957.

The abolition of slavery in 1833 led to a decline in the British population of the colonies, and the abolition of all assemblies except the oldest, Barbados. This prevented racial tension at the time, and any sense of special status by the minority. The crown agents in London were responsible for fine series of stamps, though local issues, like the Hamilton postmarks of Bermuda, and the

PLATE 29
The West Indies in the Colonial Era

307 British Guiana: the unique 1c black on magenta of 1856, currently valued at £120,000
308 French Guiana 1904, part of Inini is now an overseas department using French stamps.
309 Grenada 1953: Elizabeth II in the frame of the 1861 stamp, reintroduced in 1951.
310 Cayman Islands, a dependency of Jamaica, issued stamps in 1901. The standard colonial design for the royal Silver Wedding in 1948
311 Haiti, the western end of Hispaniola, lost control of Dominica (313) in 1844. President Simon Sam in 1898
312 Curaçao, since 1948 the Netherlands Antilles, celebrated the birth of the queen's third granddaughter in 1943. Queen Juliana and Prince Bernhard are standing (49–50).
313 Dominica, the largest of the Windward Islands, issued a farthing stamp in 1940.
314 Guadeloupe, 1940 design for the islands which have used French stamps since 1947.
315 West Indies Federation issue for Antigua 1958. Britain attempted to group small ex-colonies into viable units (354).

unique British Guiana one cent of 1856 are the most eagerly sought (307, 316). The islands resumed their strategic importance during World War II. Britain made a grant for welfare in 1943, and gave Jamaica a constitution in 1944. Special stamps were issued for this, and the opening of the British West Indian University College in 1951.

The growth of tourism helped to maintain an increasing population, but poverty drove many to emigrate to Britain where there was a labour shortage in the fifties and sixties. At the same time, there was a movement towards political independence. Britain attempted to guide this into a federation (315), but the withdrawal of Jamaica, Trinidad and Barbados as independent states within the commonwealth destroyed this experiment

PLATE 29

307

308

309

311

310

312

313

314

315

(318, 321, 323), and inevitably their economic contacts with the USA increased. The long parliamentary tradition has helped to achieve the present stability.

This left Britain, like France and the Netherlands, with the problem of the small colonies: Surinam, the two Guianas (307–8), British Honduras and the Falkland Islands (541) were unsuccessfully claimed by their large neighbours. Guyana became independent in 1966. The three powers have each devised new systems for their territories: the Fourth Republic created overseas departments in 1947 which send deputies to the French Assembly and use French stamps; the Dutch have given their colonies equal status with Holland under the crown; Britain, which changed its Colonial Office to the Commonwealth Office, and then merged it with the Foreign Office, has devised associated statehood for small territories. This involves some aid, defence, and at times police responsibilities. So great has the pressure of nationalism become, that the tiny island of Anguilla (317) seceded from St Kitts in 1967, and Metropolitan Police were called in. Detectives went to Bermuda in 1973 to investigate the assassination of the governor. The West Indies are producing interesting and attractive stamps which show their past history and present life.

The stamps of the Americas have been issued for long enough to show the roles of the different European states in the growth of the new nations. The continent is still relatively underpopulated although the energy consumption of the north is huge. The USA is bound to be of supreme importance in the area, far more than Monroe envisaged in 1823, and the two great oceans continue to inhibit large-scale foreign intervention.

316 (above) An 1854 example of the provisional issue of postmaster William B. Perot of Hamilton, Bermuda 1848–61. This Perot is valued at £50,000. Only two examples dated 1854 exist, one is in the queen's collection.

PLATE 30
The West Indies Today

317 Anguilla seceded from St Kitts–Nevis in 1967 and became a state of 6,000 people.
318 Barbados became independent in 1966. The 1972 stamp shows its role in communications.
319 The Bahamas, self-governing in 1964, became independent in 1973: girl guides issue 1970.
320 St Vincent: an associated state of Great Britain which controls the Grenadas. The 1970 issue marking twenty years of air travel, which has made tourism a major industry.
321 Trinidad and Tobago, independent since 1962, portrayed its famous carnival in 1970.
322 Barbuda, part of Antigua, issued stamps in 1922 and resumed in 1968.
323 Jamaica has had a constitution since 1944 and independence since 1962. In 1970 it honoured past leaders.

PLATE 30

ANGUILLA
METHODIST CHURCH, WEST END.
10 CENTS

317

1872-1972 TELECOMMUNICATIONS IN BARBADOS
BARBADOS EARTH STATION AND INTELSAT IV
barbados 35¢

318

(centred between 318 and 320/321)

E II R
DIAMOND JUBILEE
GIRL GUIDES
SERVICE
1910 1970
BAHAMAS
RANGERS
15

319

20TH ANNIVERSARY OF REGULAR AIR SERVICES
E II R
DOUGLAS DC3
St.Vincent 25¢

320

STEELBAND of the YEAR
Calypso King '69
Road March King '69
40¢
TRINIDAD & TOBAGO

321

61°49'
BILLY POINT
CODRINGTON VILLAGE
THE HIGHLANDS
17°35'
OYSTER POND
PALMETTO PT.
BARBUDA
½

322

NORMAN MANLEY
5 CENTS
NATIONAL HERO
Jamaica

323

CHAPTER FOUR
AFRICA AND THE MIDDLE EAST

'Winds of change' have blown more rapidly in Africa in the past century than in other parts of the world, and stamps illustrate most of the colonial expansion as well as its end. The Portuguese were the first to explore the sea route to the East, followed by the Dutch. Portugal has kept its empire, despite nationalist guerrilla movements (330–1, 362). The Dutch settled in the Cape of Good Hope in 1652, but lost it to Britain during the wars against France. In 1836 the Boer farmers trekked across the Vaal river and set up the South African Republic and then the Orange Free State (334–5). There were forts on the west coast established for the infamous slave trade, without which the Danes and the Dutch did not think it worthwhile to remain in Africa (328). The philanthropists who had ended slavery set up colonies for those wishing to return (326–7, 329). The majority of Africa still consisted of kingdoms like the Hausa Matabele, Somali and Zulu; the isolated Christian Ethiopia had a westernised emperor, Menelek, from 1888 (392), but the main influence in East Africa was Arab. The slave trade was abolished in Zanzibar only in 1873, and in 1877 Gordon was still fighting slavery in southern Egypt (382).

Interest in Africa began to revive in 1869 with the opening of the Suez Canal. In 1875 Disraeli purchased the Khedive's share, and so control of the route to India. Thus Britain assumed effective control of Egypt until 1922, leaving France to concentrate on Algeria. The pirate port had been seized in 1830, and the whole territory was made part of France after rebellion in 1871. Only in Senegal was a serious attempt being made to develop the

PLATE 31
Africa in 1880

324 Egypt: Britain purchased control of the Suez Canal in 1875, and so increased financial and political control. HP 42 airliner in 1933
325 Senegal: Louis Faideherbe, who appeared on the standard colonial design of 1906, governor 1854–64. He conquered the river basin and established groundnut farming.
326–7 Sierra Leone, 1933 issue and Gaboon were colonies for freed slaves round the capitals Freetown and Libreville.
328 Gold Coast: the Danes withdrew from forts like Christiansborg, on the 1938 design, in 1850. A colony in 1874, on the pattern of Lagos
329 Liberia: an independent state set up for freed American slaves—President Barclay 1909.
330 Angola: King Luiz on the second issue for the Portuguese colonies in 1886
331 Mozambique and Nyasa Companies were set up in 1891 and 1894 to develop the colony of 1507. Standard designs were used until 1895.
332 Cape of Good Hope: the symbol for the principal British settlement, in use 1864–93
333 Natal separated from the Cape in 1856. Edward VII on the final design in 1902
334 Orange Free State gained its independence in 1854. Its only design appeared in 1868.
335 Transvaal was ruled by the British 1877–81, but reverted to the South African Republic—the 1894 version of the arms.

PLATE 31

324

325

326

327

328

329

330

331

332

333

334

335

country for profit (325). Britain sought to protect the Zulu from the Boers, but after the defeat at Majuba Hill in 1881, accepted the Dutch independence. Colonies later came to be regarded as a nuisance, and Christian missionaries worked without government protection.

By 1900 the map of Africa had been redrawn. European nations ruled thirty-four of forty political units in the continent, and controlled four of the others. Only Liberia and Ethiopia, which defeated a modern Italian army in 1896, were fully independent. The scramble for new colonies in Africa was sparked off by personal ambition in King Leopold II of the Belgians (60) and nationalist ambition in the new Germany. Britain and France gained most from this as they were already established, and took over the German colonies in 1919 and the Italian in 1943, as spoils of war.

Leopold employed the explorer H. M. Stanley from 1879 to 1894 in the Congo basin, and in 1884 set up a Free State (336–7). The cheap, cruel management of the rubber collecting caused an international scandal, the Belgian government had to take over and the colony remained one of the most backward in Africa. Germany gained four areas: Togo, Cameroons (340), East Africa (368) and South-West Africa (346) which were recognised by the international conference of Berlin in 1884–5. These were well organised, good railways were built, but too few Germans wished to settle there.

Britain moved inland from Lagos (341–2) and set up companies to extend in southern (345) and eastern Africa (343). Heligoland (30) was given to Germany in 1889 in exchange for a free hand in Zanzibar (344). Gordon's death at Khartoum in 1884 led to Kitchener's conquest of Sudan. But the most important region was the south, where Cecil Rhodes was Prime Minister of the Cape 1890–6, and founder of the colony bearing his name (353). The discovery of diamonds and gold in the Rand had transformed

religious farming states and the Uitlanders were not allowed to become citizens. Tension led to the Jameson Raid of 1896, and then to the second Boer war in 1899. At first the Boers pinned down the British forces, as the famous and rare Mafeking siege stamps show, but after 1900 the British slowly gained con-

PLATE 32
The Scramble for Africa

336 Congo Free State, the private empire of Leopold II. Belgium took over in 1908.

337 Belgian Congo: H. M. Stanley, who explored much of central Africa, was honoured in 1928.

338 Madagascar became a French protectorate in 1890 and a colony in 1896 under Gallieni, shown on the 1932 stamp, overprinted by the free French government in 1942.

339 France occupied most of central Africa, grouped as French Equatorial Africa in 1937 and French West Africa in 1944—1914 stamp.

340 Cameroons: the German colony was divided by Britain and France in 1915. The French colony became a republic in 1960, and was joined by the southern part of the British area after a plebiscite in 1960.

341–2 Nigeria was created by the union of Lagos and the Niger Coast Protectorate, as two protectorates in 1900, and a colony in 1914.

343 East Africa was opened up by a company, and became a protectorate in 1895.

344 Zanzibar was Portuguese 1503–1730 then it fell to the Omani Arabs. It became a British protectorate in 1890; the dynasty continued till 1964. Sultan Seyyid in 1899

345 The British South Africa Company was founded by Rhodes in 1889: the arms in 1896.

346 South-West Africa, a German colony which became a South African mandate—1931 stamp.

347 Benadir, a group of coastal ports leased to Italy in 1892 which became the colony of Italian Somaliland in 1925—1903 design.

PLATE 32

336

337

338

339

340

341

342

343

344

345

346

347

trol through their unpopular concentration camp system. Peace came in 1902, and the conquest is recorded by VRI and ERI overprints, and finally by colonial issues with the royal portrait (348).

The Boers lost the war, but won the peace; in 1910 the former enemies were united as a dominion (349). As the jubilee stamp shows, all the prime ministers of the Union have been of Dutch descent (351). South Africa proved the most popular place for European emigrants.

France occupied the bulk of tropical Africa, and the Moslem island of Madagascar. A fine administration grew up under soldiers like Gallieni, Governor-General of Madagascar 1896–1905 (338), and Lyautey, who served in Indo-China and won Morocco as a French protectorate by 1912, despite German intrigues. There was full racial integration and equal education which bore fruit when a West Indian, Felix Eboué, the governor of Tchad, swung Equatorial Africa to support de Gaulle while the northern provinces were Vichy. In 1944 he inspired the important Brazzaville Conference which mapped the future of post-war African development. The colonies' stamps have borne a variety of names within the west and equatorial groupings.

European control in Africa existed in a variety of forms. Algeria was regarded as part of France and had no separate stamps until 1924 (380), Arabs were not given political rights, however, and in South Africa the Bantu lost the property qualification they had been allowed in Natal. White settlers also went to Southern Rhodesia and Kenya. The independent trading companies became either colonies or protectorates which proceeded to restrict European exploitation. The discovery of copper in Northern Rhodesia attracted an expatriate population, but otherwise there were only a few missionaries and administrators. Social and economic development took place, but there has also been a rapid rise in population.

So far as Africa was concerned, the age of imperialism meant only loose political control, in contrast to the shift of population to the old empire and USA, and to India. Pacification and administration became 'the white man's burden', and the home governments had to pay towards the often tiny staffs. After 1919 there was an even more liberal approach. The former German colonies were regarded as held in trust for the League of Nations, and the Westminster government reversed the settlement policy of Lord Delamere and insisted that Africans should have precedence in Kenya and Uganda and Tanganyika (369).

PLATE 33
Southern Africa

348 The Boer war 1899–1902: occupation overprints were issued for the two Dutch states, which became British colonies.
349 Union of South Africa set up by the amalgamation of the four colonies in 1910.
350 Bechuanaland became a protectorate in 1883 and like Basutoland and Swaziland was ruled from Britain—overprint of 1912.
351 The prime ministers of the Union on the jubilee stamp of 1960: Botha, Smuts, Hertzog, Malan, Strijdom and Verwoerd. This decimal version appeared in 1961, just prior to the declaration of the Republic.
352 The policy of apartheid led to the establishment of self-governing territories like the Transkei, whose assembly met in 1961.
353 Southern Rhodesia was self-governing from 1924, the north remained a protectorate. The Victoria Falls on the jubilee design
354 Central African Federation, set up in 1958 by a union of the colony and two former protectorates. It broke up in 1964.
355 Rhodesia made a Unilateral Declaration of Independence in 1965, so depends on South Africa and illegal trade—decimal issue 1970.
356 Basutoland became Lesotho in 1966.
357 Swaziland became independent in 1968 under King Sobhuza II.

PLATE 33

348

349

350

351

352

353

354

355

356

357

In 1923 the white settlers in Southern Rhodesia voted against joining the Union and obtained self-government, which left them in a unique constitutional position in Africa. The Union already had considerable autonomy, and in 1934 the Nationalist Government, backed by white labour with its fear of Bantu competition, asserted its sovereignty. The Depression diverted some investment to Africa and the railway system was virtually complete by 1923 (6, 9). World War II made African colonies of vital importance as primary producers, and for a time these were the sole source of revenue for the free Belgian and French governments in exile.

A number of educated and able political leaders were emerging, like Leopold Senghor of Senegal, Bourghiba the liberator and president of Tunisia and J. B. Danaqhah of the Gold Coast. The liberal element in Britain who had been opposed to colonies since the loss of America, and were regarded as 'pro-Boer' during the war, encouraged education, public health and African control, so that the French and British empires could be given away after 1951. The former Italian colony, Libya, was the first new independent power (385), and between 1955 and 1969, thirty-six new states were created.

Independence came to west Africa with no great difficulty, beginning with Ghana in 1957. It was the Mau Mau campaign in Kenya 1952–6, aimed against white settlers, which made the British accept that political freedom was to be given to her colonies. This could most easily be achieved in west Africa where there was no settled British population. The Central African Federation was an attempt to establish a multi-racial state (354), but this was no more popular than the federations in the West Indies (315) and east African independence followed. The exception was Rhodesia where there was a large white minority accustomed to self-government who followed the policy of South Africa in refusing to allow majority rule, and as no compromise formula has proved possible, Rhodesia has been an illegal state since 1965 (355).

France attempted to integrate her colonies into the Paris government by the Loi Cadre of 1956. The new assemblies wished to follow Ghana, however, but in 1958 all but Guinea voted to stay within the French community under de Gaulle. The rebel was expelled, but with help from Ghana and the USSR, took its place in the UN. This stimulated the other French colonies to seek independence, which was granted in 1960. Close links were maintained with France, and a special associate membership arranged for the European Economic Community.

PLATE 34
West Africa

358 Ivory Coast, an independent republic since 1960, has reflected French stamp designs.
359 Sierra Leone, independent since 1961, introduced self-adhesive stamps in 1964.
360 Togo became independent in 1960 after German and French rule. The President, Sylvanus Olympio, who was assassinated in 1963.
361 Nigeria celebrated the tenth year of independence, and the end of the secession of Biafra in 1970. It became a republic in 1963.
362 Angola, like Mozambique (331), has been Portuguese since the fifteenth century. Both colonies issued map designs in 1954–5.
363 Central African Republic was separated from French Equatorial Africa in 1958. The 1966 issue for the Festival of Negro Arts.
364 Congo: the French and Belgian colonies became republics in 1959–60. After the civil war and the secession of Katanga, 'Democratic' was added to the name. General Mobutu and the army took over in 1965, and the name changed to Zaire in 1971.
365 Gambia, independence issue 1965
366 Ghana, the first independent state in 1957, came under the charismatic rule of Kwame Nkrumah, born 1909, deposed 1966.

PLATE 34

358

359

360

361

362

363

364

365

366

There were tragic consequences for freedom which could be illustrated by more detailed displays of stamps. The end of colonialism in Africa has led not to nationalism, but to a return to the tribal conflicts which preceded European rule. The two most bloody examples of this have been in the Congo and Nigeria, but there has been a long and little-publicised civil war in the Sudan, and the Amin regime in Uganda is run by an army from the Moslem north.

African independence got off to a bad start with the rule of Nkrumah in Ghana, who turned the country into a one-party state and lived in archaic luxury (366). In 1963 the ruler of Togo was assassinated (360), which set an evil precedent in African politics. Nevertheless the Organisation of African Unity was set up at Addis Ababa, and made peace between Algeria and Morocco. A Liberation Committee was set up at Dar-es-Salaam in the same year which has supported guerrillas in South Africa and the Portuguese colonies, and has helped to modify western policies towards them.

Belgian Congo was given independence in 1960 without much preparation—an army mutiny provoked the secession of Katanga, which issued stamps 1960–1 under Tshombe. The radical Lumumba was arrested by the army under Mobutu (364), and later murdered in Katanga. The UN did not wish to fight, but after the death of their secretary-general (16) helped the exile Tshombe. He returned in 1964 and destroyed the rival Republique Populaire in Stanleyville. In 1965 Mobutu set up a moderate army rule.

Nigeria was created by Britain from three separate colonies, but when it became a federal state in 1960 with a booming oil industry, it should have become the richest and most stable African state. Corruption led to a southern, Ibo coup in 1966, which provoked a massacre of Ibos in the north, and the rest fled. There were threats of secession from the Moslem north, but it was the Ibos in the east who broke away as Biafra from 1967–70. For two years Biafra was supplied by air, and employed white mercenaries who had earlier fought for Katanga. The tenth anniversary of the federation marked a new, less-confident start to Nigerian life (361).

East African instability began with the deposition of the sultan of Zanzibar in 1964. Army mutinies on the mainland were put down by British troops at government request, Kenya (370) and Tanganyika under Nyerere

PLATE 35
East Africa

367 Somaliland was divided between Britain and Italy (347). This design appeared in 1942 at the same time as 'EAF' and 'BMA SOMALIA' marked Lord Wavell's conquests. Italian rule resumed in 1950 until Somalia united in 1960.

368 Tanganyika was occupied by Indian troops in 1915, and became a British mandate until 1961. There were no separate stamps from 1935 to independence.

369 Kenya, Uganda and Tanganyika had a common postal service 1935–61. Elizabeth II was proclaimed queen on the 1952 visit.

370 Kenya became independent in 1963 and a republic in 1964 under Jomo Kenyatta, born 1893.

371 Uganda became independent in 1962.

372 Tanzania was created in 1964 by the union of Tanganyika and Zanzibar.

373 Rwanda, a small republic set up in 1962 in part of the former Belgian mandate.

374 The first visit of a Pope, Paul VI, to Africa in 1969. The East African postal service is united, though separate stamps continue.

375 Malagasay, the name of Madagascar since its independence in 1958.

376 Northern Rhodesia came under Colonial Office control in 1924 (353) until 1958 (354).

377 Zambia is the name for independent Northern Rhodesia since 1964.

378 Malawi is the name for the protectorate of Nyasaland, independent since 1964.

PLATE 35

367

368

369

370

371

372

373

374

375

376

377

378

have continued peacefully (the union with Zanzibar may lead to greater stability (372)). Uganda has set an unhappy precedent by the expulsion of the Asian middle class in 1972; Ghana found it hard to replace Nkrumah and the army again exiled the liberal Busia. African politics today are like the Balkans after the end of Turkish rule, though they are more stable in the north.

Algeria was a far more acute problem to de Gaulle than West Africa. After 1945 it was treated as part of France, but the defeat in Indo-China stimulated a nationalist revolt in 1954. The army used rigorous methods, and in 1958 revolted against the government in Paris, but de Gaulle saw the impossibility of minority rule and independence followed in 1962 (384). When Colonel Boumedienne replaced Ben Bella, the FLN leader, in 1965, relations with France improved.

The whole of North Africa has moved away from Europe and reasserted its position as part of the Arab world, which reaches Indonesia and part of nationalist Africa. Egypt became an independent kingdom in 1922 (386) and Britain began to withdraw troops from 1936 under new nationalist pressure (387), but the outbreak of war turned North Africa into a battlefield. Alamein in 1942 saved Egypt from the Nazis, and was a turning point in the war. The Italians were already routed and Ethiopian independence restored (394). Italian colonies were returned in 1950, but independence soon followed (367, 385).

The weakness of Farouk's Egypt was shown by defeat in his war with the new Israel in 1948, and in 1952 he was exiled. President Nasser 1958–70, combined socialism and Islamic fervour. The nationalisation of the Suez Canal in 1956 led to a second defeat by Israel but world opinion checked the Anglo–French intervention and Russian aid developed industry. A third defeat in the Six Day War in June 1967 showed the weakness of his aggressive policies, but he had by then inspired revolts in Iraq, Libya and Yemen.

Two new features have transformed North Africa and the Middle East in the last twenty-five years—the existence of Israel and the enormous wealth brought to poor countries by oil. This wealth is mainly in Libya and the Persian Gulf, but since Qadhafi took over from the king of Libya in 1969, it has been used to support Arab and African liberation movements.

The position of Israel is unprecedented.

PLATE 36
North Africa

379 Morocco was coveted by all the colonial powers, who set up post offices. The British operated 1857–1957, though France and Spain shared protection after 1912.

380 Algeria was conquered by France in 1830. Stamps were issued 1924–45—1926 design.

381 Tunisia, a French protectorate until 1956

382 Sudan was Anglo–Egyptian 1897–1954. 1935 issue to commemorate General Gordon 1833–85.

383 Morocco, independent since 1956 and ruled by King Hassan II since 26 February 1961.

384 Algeria 'Return of peace' issue 1963

385 Libya. Italy opened a post office in 1869 and took over in 1912. King Idris I 1951–69 ruled Libya after British occupation.

Egypt
386 Fuad I, king after independence in 1922

387 Farouk, king 1937–52, on the issue for the British forces in Suez 1939

388 Revolutionary provisional 1953

389 United Arab Republic issue in 1962 for the occupation of Gaza—Israeli since 1966

390 Sudan, fully independent since 1956, and a left-wing revolution in May 1969.

391 Libyan Arab Republic under the strict army rule of Colonel Qadhafi since 1969.

PLATE 36

379

380

381

382

383

384

385

385

386

387

388

389

390

391

Judah was a puppet state in the Roman empire until the revolt of AD 66–70, when the Jews of the diaspora were left to continue the religion of Moses. Ironically the Jews were persecuted by Christians and tolerated by Arabs. Many Russian and Polish Jews went to the USA, but some settled in Turkish Palestine in the late nineteenth century. In 1917 Britain promised the Jews a national home, and at the same time independence to the Arabs under Abdulla (398) and Faisal (407). For thirty years Palestine was an uneasy mandate (395–6) with refugees from Hitler trying to smuggle themselves in, and terrorists harrying the British army. Finally in 1948 Israel was established with financial support from the USA and massive sympathy from a Europe sickened by Hitler's genocide (397).

This created a Palestinian refugee problem, which has increased since. Israel has fought four brilliant defensive wars against her neighbours, who refuse to recognise her and support Palestinian guerrillas. She occupies areas of Egypt and Jordan pending a settlement. The Soviet Union supports the Arabs, who are using their oil as a lever to turn the USA from supporting Israel. Jordan, the only kingdom to survive, apart from the desert Saudi-Arabia, retains links with Britain. It is possible that combined USA and Soviet pressure might bring about peace.

To the north of Israel, Syria was a kingdom under Faisal 1918–20, and bitterly opposed the French mandate. There have been a series of regimes since 1946. The Syrian Arab Republic set up in 1961 survived a revolution in 1963. Lebanon, the ancient Phoenician trading area, became an independent political unit for the first time in 1946. Beirut was the major city in the Levant (104–7) and suffered badly from the Turks 1915–18, when the EEF occupied it (395). The French mandate was followed by a democracy based on religious allegiance; a similar system has worked less well in Cyprus where there is still strong pressure for union with Greece (403).

Turkey, which had once ruled much of Asia and Africa, almost ceased to exist after 1918. Mohammed VI ruled 1918–22, with the allies in Constantinople and the Greeks in Smyrna. A republic was set up by Mustapha Kemal (401) and the Greek army was expelled, though the city did not recover. Kemal ruled as dictator till 1938 and westernised Turkey who fought with the UN in Korea, and is a member of NATO. Its stability still depends

PLATE 37
Ethiopia, Palestine, the Levant

Ethiopia
392 Menelek defeated Italy in 1896 and modernised the country—issue of 1909.
393 Italy conquered in 1936 and joined it to Eritrea and Italian Somaliland in 1938.
394 Haile Selassie, emperor since 1930, drove the Italians out in 1941—the 1942 design. Eritrea joined Ethiopia in 1952.

Palestine
395 Egyptian Expeditionary Force design of 1918 overprinted for the British mandate.
396 The Dome of the Rock on the 1927 series
397 Israel 1955: the Lion of Judah
398 Emir, later King, Abdullah on the 1927 design for the British mandate Transjordan
399 Jordan became a kingdom in 1946. Hussein became king in 1952, when Talal was deposed.

The Levant
400 Syria was a French mandate 1920–42, then a republic. Part of the UAR (389) 1958–61
401 Turkey became a modern state under Kemal Ataturk, president 1922–38, portrayed in 1970.
402 Lebanon was a French mandate 1920–41. The 1967 stamp for the International Tourist Year
403 Cyprus: a bilingual overprint marked independence in 1960. Racial tension continues.

PLATE 37

392

393

394

395

396

397

398

399

400

401

402

403

on the professional army and the American alliance.

Indian troops conquered Iraq in 1914–17; their progress is marked by stamps for Baghdad, Basra and Mosul. Union with India was considered, but after the mandate of 1920 a nationalist revolt led to the Faisal, Ameer of Damascus, being made king. In 1932 Iraq joined the League of Nations, but the British bases continued until 1958. Under the young King Ghazi, and his infant son, there were a series of coups, and in 1941 there was a pro-German government. The treaty with Britain was abrogated in 1955 and a union with Jordan set up, but in 1958 Brigadier Kassem murdered the royal family. His execution was shown on television in 1963, but a further army coup followed in the same year.

Saudi-Arabia, which became a stable state in 1932, contains the Moslem Holy City, Mecca, to which thousands of pilgrims travel each year (20). A portrait of the new King Faisal appeared in 1964, marking the end of the religious taboo.

The Yemen won freedom from Turkey in 1911 though this was not recognised until 1918. The Imam Yahya ruled until he was shot in 1948, but a counter-coup established his heir, Ahmed. The Yemen Arab Republic was set up in 1962, but the royalists continued to resist, despite Egyptian aid, and have been partly financed by stamps (413).

Aden became important as a coaling station after the opening of the Suez Canal. Britain established protectorates over neighbouring sultanates, and in the post-colonial era tried to set up a South Arabian Federation in 1965. Civil war followed between the conservatives of the desert and the socialists of the city, and the army was occupied in trying to maintain order until a People's Republic of Southern Yemen was established in 1967. Despite the similar names, this is still separate from the Arab republic. With the increase in the size of ships and the closing of the Suez Canal in the 1967 war, the Red Sea is less important as a trade route.

This chapter has covered two distinct cultures, the Arab and the African. The two linked in the French and British empires after the defeat of Turkey, and they are now regarded as part of the third, or 'developing' world, in contrast to the western and soviet blocs. Islam made many converts in Nigeria, the Sudan and Uganda, and the continuing apartheid in South Africa has damaged Christianity. Most of the new states are attempting rapid progress towards an urban way of life, without the raw materials or skills to support this. It is possible that the 'cradle of civilisation' may again lead the world in communal living.

PLATE 38
Arabia

Saudi-Arabia was separated from Turkey in 1916. The Sultan of Nejd conquered Hejaz in 1926, and adopted the present name in 1932.
404 Mecca hospital on the 1936 charity stamp
405 Gas oil plant on the 1960 design
406 Iraq was occupied by Britain in World War I. Overprint on Turkey 1918 prior to the granting of the mandate in 1920. This led to a war of independence.
407 Faisal became king in 1921, after being driven from Syria. Abdullah of Jordan (398) had been king in 1920, Ghazi ruled 1933–9.
408 Faisal II, born 1935, assassinated 1958, shown with the republican overprint.
409 Pan-Arab games, Baghdad 1971
Aden was conquered in 1839, but used Indian stamps 1854–1937. It was a vital harbour.
410 The final colonial series 1953
411 Sultan Hussein 1954, on one of the states united in the South Arabian Federation in 1965.
412 The Yemen People's Democratic Republic was set up as Southern Yemen in 1967. Yemen was ruled by an Imam 1926–62 when it became the Yemen Arab Republic.
413 The north has continued as an Islamic kingdom and issues a great number of stamps.

PLATE 38

404

405

406

407

408

409

410

411

412

413

CHAPTER FIVE

ASIA

One vital element in the opening up of Asia to European influence cannot be shown in stamps. From the late eighteenth century Russia pushed her frontiers eastwards and included central Asian tribes in her empire. Her frontiers eventually marched with China and brought her into fatal conflict with the new, aggressive Japan. Britain saw Russia as a threat to India through Afghanistan, but it was in Persia that the two imperial powers came near to conflict. Russia failed to restore the deposed shah in 1910 (414) but succeeded in making a treaty with cossack leader Riza Khan in 1921. Britain drew much of her oil from Persia, and growing German influence led to a joint Anglo–Russian invasion in 1941, to protect supplies. The new shah co-operated and received Azerbaijan as a reward in 1946, marked by special stamps in 1950. In 1951 the nationalist government of Dr Mussadeq nationalised oil, commemorated in 1953, and expelled British staff. This was a severe blow to Britain, but relations began to improve under General Zahedi who took power in 1953, and the queen visited the shah in 1961.

British interest moved to the small Gulf states which had been incidental spoils in the nineteenth century, administered from India. Special stamps were issued in place of overprints in 1960, and in 1966 the independent states set up their own post offices. Britain retains special interest in the area. Several tiny sheikdoms have stamps produced commercially to provide some income (423–4).

The other area of Anglo–Russian conflict was the mountain state of Afghanistan. There were unsuccessful British invasions in 1839–40 and 1879–80, but Britain had effective

PLATE 39
The Persian Gulf

Iran was westernised under Nasr-ed-Din who reigned 1848–96. His successor, Muzaffer-el-Din, granted a constitution in 1906.

414 Muhammad Ali 1907–9 revoked the reforms and controlled only Teheran. Russian troops attempted to restore him in 1910–11 but anarchy continued until after the war.

415 Riza Sha Pahlavi the cossack commander, seized Teheran in 1921. He replaced Shah Ahmed in 1925—his portrait in 1929.

416 In 1935 the name Iran was adopted. In 1941 Shah Muhammed Riza Pahlavi replaced his father.

Bahrain came under British control in 1820 in an anti-slavery campaign, and was occupied 1914.

417 Indian stamps were used 1884–1933, when overprints were made.

418 The British post office took over in 1948.

419 British post office issue of 1948

420 Local control was established in 1959. The Sheik Sir Abdullah in 1964, died 1965. Muscat and Oman had Indian post from 1864.

421 Portraits of the sheiks appeared in 1960 and in 1966 the local post office took control. The first VC 10 flight from the Gulf in 1970. Kuwait used Indian stamps and overprints.

422 The name was reduced to Oman in 1971.

423 Fujeira is a poor trucial state which has had stamps produced by an agency since 1964.

424 Dubai had an Indian post from 1909 and British stamps from 1948. Stamps were produced in Beirut 1963–7, when the government took over.

PLATE 39

414

415

416

417

418

419

420

421

422

423

424

control 1907–18. Since then regular stamp issues have celebrated Afghan independence. From 1959–63 it encouraged the Pathans to leave Pakistan, but failed despite Russian support. Kabul is now a popular centre for western youth trying to escape from the pressures of civilisation.

On the north-east frontier of India, Tibet which issued only thirteen stamps in the years 1912–33, was taken over by China in 1950. Nine years later there was a revolt in Lhasa, and the Dalai Lama fled to India with many followers, provoking the Chinese invasion of India. Tibet is now more cut off from the west than before. Nepal, on the other hand, settled its frontier with China in 1961. The land of Everest (442), and Britain's mercenary Ghurka army, it had two series of stamps in 1881 and 1907, but in 1948 regular issues began.

These independent kingdoms are a reminder that India was created by Britain from a large collection of principalities. In 1799 'John Company' controlled only the Ganges Delta and part of the coast. France was negotiating with Tipu of Mysore to recover her control. By 1833 the East India Company had become a government and brilliant leaders like the two Lawrence brothers had extended the *Pax Britannica* over most of the subcontinent. A new type of sober, evangelical officer suppressed the crueller aspects of Hinduism and encouraged Christianity. However, the mutiny of 1857, which was largely confined to the Bengal army and led to the dropping of the company title (438), undermined British confidence and there were no more annexations. The 700 remaining states continued until they were grouped in 1948. Forty of them issued stamps, mainly from 1866–1900, but Bahawalpur in Pakistan did so only 1945–50 (435).

In 1877 Disraeli made Victoria Empress of India and reinstituted the ancient Durbars. Lord Curzon, the viceroy 1898–1905 was almost too regal, but was impartial and just in the best imperial tradition. The jubilee issue of George V reflected the splendour of India (440). More important was the establishment of the cotton, jute and tea industries and some means of famine control. The Congress Party was encouraged before 1900, but after 1914 its demands escalated in Gandhi's (445) passive resistance campaigns. Legislation in 1919 and 1935 paved the way to self-government, but from 1937 Jinnah's

PLATE 40
Indian Monarchies

425 Afghanistan has preserved its freedom despite British and Russian intrigues. An airport was opened at Kabul in 1964. It became a republic in 1973.

426 Nepal used Indian stamps for foreign mail 1881–1959. King Mahendra, acceded 1955, is shown with the east-west highway 1964.

427 Jaipur issued stamps from 1904 until it became part of Rajasthan in 1948.

428 Gwalior, now in Madhya Pradesh, issued stamps 1885–1949 within a postal convention.

429 Patiala, a Sikh member of the convention

430 Indore issued stamps 1886–1947, until 1904 identified by the dynastic name: Holkar XII 1889.

431 Hyderabad issued stamps 1869–1949.

432 Charkhari joined Vindhya Pradesh in 1948 but used its own stamps 1894–1950: 1931 stamp.

433 Travancore issued stamps 1888–1950. It joined to Cochin and became Kerala in 1956: the Maharajah Sir Bala Rama Varma in 1939.

434 Soruth issued stamps in 1887. It used the name Saurashtra after 1929 and became Gujaret in 1960—official overprint on the 1929 issue.

435 Bahawalpur issued official stamps from 1945 and, after a brief independence in 1947, joined Pakistan. Stamps appeared until 1950. The jubilee in 1949 of the Nawab Sadiq Muhammed Khan V 1924–68, a renowned philatelist.

PLATE 40

425

426

427

428

429

430

431

432

433

434

435

Moslem League insisted on partition on religious grounds. The war delayed moves towards autonomy, but division proved the only solution in 1947–8, and the birth of the two new nations was marred by bloodshed between the two religions.

India was governed by Pandit Nehru until 1964. He attempted to establish a neutral policy and continue the peaceful democratic methods of Gandhi. The tiny French colonies were assimilated, but the Portuguese had to be driven from Goa in 1961 (447). He was intransigent about the Moslem state of Kashmir. Pakistan claimed this and there was a major frontier war in 1965. China had infiltrated, and Russia sought to mediate. Nehru gained nothing by propitiating China and lost American support. His daughter, Mrs Gandhi, has continued his policy since 1966 and supported the secession of Bangladesh in 1971 (454). India has made rapid industrial progress and attempted to limit population.

The creation of the Dominion of Pakistan in two sections was a last-minute compromise. In 1956 it became a republic, but remained in the British commonwealth, as India had done in 1950. In 1959 a military coup made General Ayub Khan president. Tension between Pakistan and India has continued, despite the proximity of China. There were persistent complaints by the Bengalis that the west was favoured, and in 1971 the east revolted under Sheikh Mujibar Rahman, who with Indian help set up the new state of Bangladesh. In 1954 Pakistan joined SEATO (270), and in 1964 made a regional Development Pact with Turkey and Iran (436–7). In 1972 she left the British commonwealth, and relations with Afghanistan have been better since 1963.

India was the springboard for the British occupation of Burma in three stages, 1824, 1852 and 1907. Although it was treated as part of the empire until 1937, Burma was never fully anglicised. Its first stamps marked the granting of self-government as a crown colony (448); in World War II it became a battlefield. The Japanese invaded from Vichy

436–7 (above) Pakistan 1969: the fifth anniversary of the Regional Co-operation for Development, showing Persian and Ottoman art.

PLATE 41
India

438 The archaic East India inscription as used 1855–66. The 1882 series reverted to the title used on the first stamps in 1854.

439 The Victorian designs were repeated for Edward VII as the emperor in 1902.

440 The Taj Mahal on the jubilee issue 1935

441 The first definitive series of the new dominion, in 1949, portrayed Hindu culture.

442 India became a republic in 1950: the 1953 issue for the first ascent of Everest.

443 The jubilee of the Indian Air Force in 1958 is a reminder of the threats to peace.

444 The atomic reactor on the 1965 series indicates India's rapid industrial progress.

445 Mahatma Gandhi 1869–1948, was portrayed in the year of his assassination to mark the first anniversary of independence.

446 The Free French issue in 1942 for the small French territories which joined the republic 1952–4.

447 1953 issue for the Portuguese colony, which was taken over in 1961.

PLATE 41

438

439

440

441

442

443

444

445

446

447

Indo-China and drove an inadequate British garrison back to India (449). Some nationalists in both countries supported the invaders, India was held and the British army learned how to excel at jungle warfare, with an army and an air force operating behind Japanese lines. Burma was recaptured after a bitter campaign in 1944–5 (450). In 1947 she decided to leave the commonwealth, and after a period of violence the new Union of Burma came into existence. U Thant was secretary-general of the United Nations 1960–7.

Ceylon, like Burma, is Buddhist, but has had more European influence. Britain gained it from the Dutch in 1803 and took over Kandy in 1815 (456). It remained a crown colony until 1948. The assassination of the Prime Minister Mr S. W. R. D. Bandaranaike in 1959 showed the violence that has been a continual threat. His wife became the first woman premier in the world, and in 1972 her party adopted the name Sri Lanka.

Britain also ruled the Maldive Islands, Seychelles and Mauritius in the Indian Ocean. In 1965 a new colony, the British Indian Ocean Territory, was created to provide a base on Gan. Since 1971 British forces have been withdrawn from Asia, apart from the Hong Kong garrison. The first Mauritius stamps are the most sought after in the world as only a thousand were printed, of which twenty-six survive (458).

The French empire in Asia was mainly in Indo-China. Napoleon III had invaded Annam, but the Third Republic withdrew until 1878. It took until 1913 to subjugate the empire of Vietnam, which consisted of Tonkin, Annam and Cochin-China, and the kingdoms of Laos and Cambodia. A resistance movement was established in Tokyo in 1905 and independence was promised in 1944. France established the rubber and coal industries and built Saigon as a fine European city. The stamps of the thirties portrayed regional leaders, and the opening of the railway was marked in 1938 (462). The colonial government supported Pétain and in 1940 allowed

Japan to establish bases to attack Burma.

The communist leader Ho Chi Minh formed the Viet Minh in China with American support. This opposed both Japanese and French, and in 1946 seized control from the Japanese and set up the Democratic Republic of North Vietnam. The British used Japanese prisoners to police the south, and quickly handed over to France, which decided to reconquer. In 1946 Ho Chi Minh attacked Hanoi and the long agony began.

The primary policy of the Viet Minh was nationalist. The French reintroduced the states of Vietnam, Laos and Cambodia in

PLATE 42
The Indian Sub-Continent

Burma was separated from India in 1937.
448 Posthumous overprint on George V
449 Japanese occupation issue 1943
450 British military administration issue 1945, on the definitive design of 1937 and 1946. Burma became an independent republic in 1948.

Pakistan
451 Provisional overprint of 1947
452 The disputed area of Kashmir 1960
453 Ninth anniversary of independence 1956
454 Bangladesh, formerly East Pakistan, was set up in 1970. First anniversary of independence 1972

Indian Ocean
455 Maldive Islands, a British protectorate, issued stamps in 1906. It was a republic in 1953 and since 1968. The ninth anniversary of the sultan in 1962. Independent since 1965
456 Ceylon: the 1935 and 1938 definitive
457 D. S. Senanayake, prime minister on the first anniversary of independence set 1949
458 Mauritius: the rare 1847 twopence blue 'post office', now worth £40,000 mint. The 1848 issue was correctly engraved 'post paid'.
459 Self-government was granted in 1967 and independence in the following year.

PLATE 42

448

449

450

451

452

453

454

455

456

457

458

459

1949, but in that year China became communist and provided the support which was to lead to the victory at Dien Bien Phu just before the international conference met at Geneva to settle the problem in 1954 (465). France withdrew, and the puppet emperor Bao Dai invited Ngo Dinh Diem to form a government. The country was partitioned, Diem (467) became president in the south but with a large communist underground. For five years there was peaceful progress, then in 1959 a new communist attack began. Diem fell in 1963, and after a year of chaos the USA moved in and checked the communist progress. They were unable to defeat the north by bombing, and in 1973 they withdrew in return for a delicate peace settlement. The war continued in neighbouring Cambodia, and co-existence as it has evolved in Germany is still a long way off in south-east Asia.

Thailand, which lies between Burma, Vietnam and the Malay peninsula managed to avoid being dominated by a European power. The royal family had a postal service with very early photographically produced stamps before the public service began in 1883. There was a brief French occupation in 1894 which led to some territory being granted to Indo-China, and four Malay states to Britain (473). Bulk mail from Chinese immigrants required high value stamps in 1907-8. The Thai air force fought in France and the contract to print stamps had to be transferred to London from Austria (469). Airmail flights began in 1920.

A strong nationalist government deposed King Prajadhipok in 1935, and in 1941 the name Siam was dropped. The Japanese were allowed to invade Malaya through Thailand in return for the states lost in 1894, and British prisoners were used to build a trans-Thailand railway. Only four stamps appeared 1942-7 (470). Since the war Thailand has been a major air route and become a member of SEATO. USA influence has been considerable, and many of the air offensives against North Vietnam used Thailand bases. Thailand

has the advantage of no frontier with China.

Malaya at the beginning of the nineteenth century was part of the sphere of the Dutch East Indies. Britain occupied these in the Napoleonic wars, and Stamford Raffles 1781-1826, had the vision of a British Malaya. As an official of the East India Company, he took Singapore in 1819 and founded one of the most important trading points in the world, and a vital link in the British empire. Malaya's fall to the Japanese in 1942 was the greatest disaster in British military history and even more than the Japanese defeat of Russia marked the end of European supremacy. With Malacca and Penang, a crown colony was established in 1867 (472). Separate stamps did not appear until 1948, in the pre-war Straits Settlements design.

With its large Chinese population and

PLATE 43
Indo-China

460 The French resumed conquest in 1878, and by 1913 controlled all but Thailand (1892).

461 The 1907-22 design of an Annamite woman used on the Chinese island Kouang-Tcheou.

462 1938 opening of the trans-Indo-China railway. Paul Doumer 1857-1932, began the development of the colony as governor. He was assassinated as president of France.

463 Cambodia became an associated state in 1954, independent 1954-5 and the Khmer Republic in 1971—definitive of 1954.

464 Laos has been an independent kingdom since 1949 and issued stamps since 1951. Air set of 1957 commemorating Buddhism

465 North Vietnam 1957 issue to mark the twelfth anniversary of the republic.

466 Tenth anniversary of the liberation of Hanoi from the French, 1964

467 South Vietnam: Ngo Dinh Diem president 1955 and 1961, killed in the military coup of 1963.

468 Asian Productivity Year 1970

PLATE 43

460

461

462

463

464

465

466

467

468

distinct tradition, Singapore could not fit into the Malayan Federation, and in 1965 it became an independent republic within the British commonwealth (480).

Britain occupied the mainland of Malaya by 1914, when Johore was incorporated. The first move was to protect the Perak tin mines in 1871, which involved a minor war in 1875. Residents advised the rajahs, which involved creating governments. The federated states became a base for further expansion (474) and Siam recognised British control in the north in return for a loan. Rubber seeds were smuggled from Brazil in 1876 and after 1910 the industry boomed and became a major aim for the Japanese expansion in World War II.

The Japanese occupation (475) left the same legacy of communist and nationalist guerrillas as in Indo-China and the Indies. Britain won the war which lasted 1948-60, as there was no frontier with China, and careful control accompanied rapid economic recovery. The formation of the multi-racial Alliance Party in 1953 paved the way for independence in 1957 and the end of the terrorist threat. This was followed by a confrontation with the aggressive Indonesia from 1963-6.

The spices of the East Indies had been the goal of the earliest European voyages. The new Dutch republic won control in the seventeenth century against Spain and England. This was by far the most valuable possession in their empire, but had only a small Dutch population. Few Javanese and Sumatrans were educated and Chinese and Eurasians made up the middle class. Nationalist groups began after 1905 and in 1926 the Partai Kommunist Indonesia launched an unsuccessful revolt which failed to attract the devout Moslem peasants. Communism was suppressed and in 1927 Sukarno (484) helped to found the Partai National Indonesis. The revolt retarded progress. The Japanese were welcomed by the imprisoned nationalists in 1942, Dutch was banned and Sukarno and his party were allowed to run the country. When the Japanese withdrew in 1945 Sukarno declared

Indonesia to be an independent republic. The British occupation force needed Japanese aid to control the nationalists, despite their low-key approach and the Dutch were faced with a major war in 1947-8, which was very unpopular with the UN and the USA. The republic continued to operate, and issued its own stamps. Dutch attempts to establish a federation failed (483) by the end of 1949.

PLATE 44
Thailand and Malaya

469 King Vijiravudh 1912–26. This issue was printed in London from 1914 instead of Vienna, after Siam fought with Britain and France.

470 1943 locally produced issue during the Thai collaboration with the Japanese.

471 King Bhumibol Adulyadej succeeded his brother Ananda Mahidol in 1946.

472 The Straits Settlements: Singapore, Malacca and Penang became a crown colony in 1867. Labuan was added 1906–41, and joined North Borneo in 1946.

473 Kelantan, Kedah, Perlis and Trengganu were ceded to Britain by the Anglo–Siamese Treaty of 1909, and apart from Perlis, issued stamps from 1911. Siam recovered them 1942–6.

474 Negri Sembilan, Pahang, Perak and Selangor united as the Federated Malay States in 1896. In 1935 they joined the Malayan Postal Union and separate issues were resumed.

475 General issue by the Japanese 1943

476 British military administration 1945, operated throughout the peninsula.

477 Perak 1950, Sultan Yussuf Izzudin Shah

478 Malayan Federation established in 1957 by the combination of the states with Penang and Malacca. Singapore remained independent.

479 Malaysia was formed in 1963 by the addition of Sabah, Sarawak and Singapore. The tenth anniversary of federation in 1967

480 Singapore became a republic in 1965.

PLATE 44

469

470

471

472

473

474

475

476

477

478

479

480

Indonesia began with an ideal constitution for which it was unprepared. The Korean war brought prosperity, but by 1959 Sukarno had taken supreme power. Dutch New Guinea was incorporated in 1962, but pressure against the incorporation of Sabah and Sarawak into the new Malaysia led to raids and withdrawal from the UN in 1965. A communist revolt led to the fall of Sukarno and the suppression of the PKI.

The two areas claimed by Indonesia were parts of Borneo and New Guinea. James Brooke was made rajah of Sarawak in 1841 by the sultan of Brunei, which remains under British protection. Brooke destroyed the Dayak pirates and paved the way for the North Borneo Company, which introduced pictorial stamps in 1894 among its other profitable activities. Both areas reverted to the crown in 1946, after the Japanese had been driven out. New Guinea was divided into three until 1918, when Australia took over. It was the extent of the Japanese advance on Australia, and a key battle area in World War II (486).

The Indies were the limit of European and Moslem expansion, and the two great Asian civilisations had little contact with Europe until the nineteenth century, apart from small trading posts in China. The war to protect the British opium trade from 1839 to 1842 led to Hong Kong becoming a colony and Kowloon was added in 1860. It continues as a unique point of contact with China (498). The Dowager Tz'u-hsi manipulated the emperor and allowed the fanatical sect of the Boxers to massacre Europeans. A combined force defeated them with a lot of Chinese support and by 1900 China was defenceless, but not dismembered as so many powers were involved (495–7).

In 1891 the Christian, Sun Yat-sen (492–9), founded the nationalist Kuomintang. In 1911 he joined the revolution against the emperor and was elected president of the republic in Nanking. He handed over power to General Yuan Shi Kai who had persuaded the young Pu-Yi to abdicate, and who became president, and then emperor, until his death in 1916. The Nanking Constitution was restored, but such was the power of the war lords that the Kuomintang did not achieve power until after the death of its founder. Chiang Kai-shek won control 1926–8 and adopted a modern constitution in 1931. He had already begun to quarrel with the large communist party and, with Russian support, began to destroy them. This led to Mao Tse-tung's heroic 'Long March' in 1935 to the safety of Shenshi. The USA supported Chiang Kai-shek, and Christian missions played a growing part in China. The Japanese invasion in 1937 was resisted by both parties, who continued to fight each other. By 1938 Japan controlled much of the north and centre, and in 1940 made Britain close the Burma supply road. The only response from the USA to the

PLATE 45
The East Indies

Indonesia
481 Dutch standard colonial issue 1912
482 Salvation Army charity issue 1936
483 Dutch Indonesia issue 1949
484 Indonesian Republic established 1950. President Sukarno in 1951, born 1901
485 1969: computer operator on the five-year development plan second series

486 Papua and New Guinea 1952 definitive issue for the former German and British parts administered by Australia, but claimed by Indonesia.
487 Brunei, Sultan Omar Ali Saifuddin 1952
488 Sarawak, Sir Charles Vyner Brooke the last white rajah, 1918–41 and 1946, when he handed the island over to the crown.
489 Malaysian standard issue of 1965
490 North Borneo became a protectorate in 1909: the sultan of Sulu with his staff and the chairman of the British Company.
491 North Borneo joined Malaysia in 1963 and was renamed Sabah in 1964—1961 map overprinted.

PLATE 45

481

482

483

484

485

486

487

488

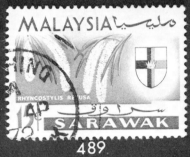

489

490

491

Japanese advance was to move the fleet to Pearl Harbour in 1940. Once war was declared, the USA flew supplies to China.

During the war, communist guerrillas were very successful behind the Japanese lines. The end of the war found Japan in control, except in Manchuria, which Russia took in the final week. Chiang Kai-shek claimed to be ruler of China, and as he had larger forces and an air force, the USA expected the communists to join his government. A short truce was followed by communist seizure of Manchuria. By 1947 the nationalists were in retreat and their economy was collapsing. The battle of Huai Hai in 1949 led to total victory in 1950, with only Taiwan remaining to the nationalists.

Mao Tse-tung won a remarkable victory by discipline, opposed to superior weapons and air power. It seemed as though world communism was dominant, though its further advance was stopped in the Korean war. The Five Year Plan of 1953 was financed by Russia, but differences in approach emerged. The Great Leap Forward in 1958 asserted China's claim to lead world communism, and though the Cultural Revolution of 1966 slowed economic growth, Mao's peasant-based system has more to offer to Asia and Africa. There are border conflicts between China and Russia, and each has opened relations with the USA in order to preserve peace. The USA maintained the fiction that Chiang was the legal ruler of China until 1972, when it was recognised as a member of the United Nations.

Japan was forcibly opened to western influence by the American Commodore Perry in 1854. Frantic modernisation began under the Emperor Meiji, who overthrew the shogunate in 1868. Postage stamps in 1871 and a railway in 1872 were steps in the industrialisation that prepared the army and navy to smash the Chinese in 1894–5, seize the puppet empire of Korea (511) and block further Russian progress by taking Port Arthur. Russian diplomatic pressure forced Japan to return Liaotung and allow a lease on Port Arthur in 1898, giving Russia effective

control of Manchuria (497). This paved the way for the war of 1904–5 in which a European power was defeated by an Asian. Japan was the dominant power in the Far East, though Britain took Weihaiwei and France Kouang-Tcheou (461) for their diplomatic support. Japan supported the allies during World War I and from 1918–22 occupied eastern Siberia.

Britain resumed the Japanese alliance in 1919 and Japanese trade blossomed in China.

PLATE 46
China

492 1912 revolution series portraying Dr Sun Yat Sen 1867–1925, president in Nanking 1911.

493 1898 imperial definitive issue

494 1912 series portraying President Yuan Shih Kai who persuaded the emperor to abdicate.

495 China Expeditionary Force overprint for the use of Indian troops sent to suppress the Boxer Rising 1900–13.

496 Japanese post offices operated in the same period—the 1913 issue.

497 Russian post offices operated 1899–1920.

498 Hong Kong: a major port and industrial centre. The Annigoni portrait of Queen Elizabeth II 1962

499 Sun Yat-sen portrayed in 1931, became the symbol of the republic under the Kuomintang.

500 Chiang Kai-shek on the victory issue 1945

501 Formosa 1955: celebrating Chiang Kai-shek's sixty-ninth birthday

The communist forces issued many stamps for areas under their control after 1929. These mark their progress against the nationalists.

502 South China 1949: liberation of Canton

503 Chinese People's Republic 1954: thirtieth anniversary of the death of Lenin, born 1870

504 East China 1949: Mao Tse-tung, born 1893

PLATE 46

492

493

494

495

496

497

498

499

500

501

502

503

504

USA pressure forced the return of Shantung and limited the Japanese fleet, which in turn encouraged the growth of militarist groups. The USA was nervous of Japan, but also afraid of a strong China. The slump hit Japan's economy and led to the occupation of Manchuria in 1931, against the emperor's orders. Pu-yi was made emperor of a puppet state Manchuko (506). In response to world criticism, Japan left the League of Nations in 1933 and attacked China in 1937 and the USA in 1941. By the end of 1942 Japan controlled Burma and the Pacific, ensuring vital supplies of oil and rubber. The USA carrier victory at Midway stemmed the advance, however, and the war began to turn in the allies' favour. The use of the atomic bomb in 1945 is generally criticised, but the conventional invasion of China and Japan would have been very costly in human life.

The Emperor Hirohito continued as head of state and the USA set out to rebuild Japan. Post-war stamps reflected austerity and effort. A peace treaty was signed in 1951: Japan was not allowed to rearm, but was free to build up her industry and export to the USA. The economic miracle of the nineteenth century was repeated, and Japan is now among the most wealthy powers in the world. Stamps reflect ancient culture and national parks, but also the Tokyo–Osaka railway in 1964 and atomic power in 1965. The royal visit to Europe in 1971 (509–10) marked the achievement of as great a standing by trade as by war. There are left-wing movements in Japan, and relations with the heavily armed China have to be worked out.

The old area of conflict, Korea, was split into two republics in 1948: two years later the north invaded the south. As the USSR had left the Security Council, the UN was able to intervene and by October had reached the Yalu River. At this point China came in and pushed the UN south. A counter-attack led to stalemate on the forty-ninth parallel, and the frontier was confirmed in the peace of 1953. South Korea has flourished under USA protection and this success was a precedent for intervention in the more complex situation in Vietnam (512–3).

As soon as the federal government was established on the west coast, the USA realised how weak her long Pacific seaboard was—hence the annexation of Hawaii in 1896 (514) and the conquest of the Spanish Philippines in 1898, despite the anti-imperialist tradition. Political development was encouraged from 1926. MacArthur's army held out in Bataan until May 1942. The Japanese occupation was unpopular, and guerrillas paved the way for the liberation 1944–5. Full independence followed in 1946 but the USA retains naval and air control in the area.

PLATE 47
Japan and the North Pacific

Japan
505 English inscriptions were used only 1876–96 and since 1966.
506 Manchukuo was set up as a puppet state in 1932. Issue to mark the visit of Pu-Yi, the emperor, to Japan in 1940.
507 Wartime definitive series 1942
508 Imperforate definitive of 1946
509–10 Japan as a major world power. The visit of the Emperor Hirohito to Europe in 1971, which incorporates a painting by his wife.

Korea
511 1895 issue of the empire, independent under Chinese influence until 1910. It then used Japanese stamps until 1946.
512 South Korea: Hibiscus on the 1953 definitive
513 North Korea: 1965 Seven-Year Plan

Pacific Ocean
514 Hawaii was an independent kingdom until 1893. The USA annexed it in 1896. 1864 portrait of King Kamehameha V
515 Philippine Islands were ceded to the USA by Spain in 1898. Definitive series 1906
516 Self-government was granted in 1936 and independence in 1946 after the Japanese occupation of 1941–5. 1965 stamp

PLATE 47

505

506

507

508

509

510

511

512

513

514

515

516

CHAPTER SIX

AUSTRALASIA AND THE ANTARCTIC

Captain Cook had explored the South Seas, and in 1787 convicts and soldiers had been sent to Botany Bay. Thirty-five years later men began to explore the land and to settle and farm. Victoria split from New South Wales in 1850, and Queensland in 1859. The act of 1850 marked the end of convicts, except in the deserted western territory. The seal of New South Wales appeared on its stamps in 1850, while the constitution followed in 1855. Western Australia issued stamps in 1854, but received its constitution only in 1870 when the last sentences had been served.

Progress was slower in New Zealand as Maori wars smouldered until 1870. The colony was given authority in 1862, and six years later added four Maoris to their Assembly.

Gold drew settlers to the colonies, the clippers accelerated the wool trade, and steam refrigeration and Suez stimulated stock farms. Tariffs protected industry, and the jubilee in 1897 stimulated the ideals of federation and empire. Politics had been volatile, there was little communication, but in 1901 the Commonwealth of Australia came into being. New Zealand obtained dominion status in 1907, and so inscribed her stamps 1909–13 (517–9). Like the USA, it is easy to trace the history of both dominions through centenary stamps, which began as early as 1888.

Defence relied on small contributions to the British navy, but after the London Imperial Conference of 1911, joint planning paved the way for the ANZAC contribution to World War I, which was again marked

by stamps in 1969 (87). The sons of convicts and exiles developed pride and a sense of identity, but the determined 'white Australia' policy of 1888 directed against Chinese, meant that the population was only 7 million in 1939, and less than 12 million in 1966, instead of the 30 million predicted before 1900.

PLATE 48
The Colonial Era in Australia

520 New South Wales: 1888 centenary of Captain Phillip's settlement at Sydney
521 South Australia 1895: the kangaroo
522 Victoria 1901: redrawn 1890 design
523 Western Australia 1885: the final form of the famous black swan emblem
524 Queensland 1860: the beautiful Humphreys' engraving of the first issue
525 Tasmania 1899: Mount Wellington on an early pictorial series without portrait
526 Commonwealth of Australia 1913: this famous design last appeared in 1946.
527 New Zealand 1900: commemoration of the Boer War contingent

517–19 (below) New Zealand 1907 and 1909 issues mark the progress from colony to dominion. The penny stamp also indicates the world-wide imperial postage rate, part of the imperial ideal (282).

PLATE 48

520

521

522

523

524

525

526

527

At Versailles, Australia received German New Guinea as a colony (486) and New Zealand gained Samoa (540). The Imperial Conference of 1926 declared the equality of dominions and Britain, enshrined in the 1931 State of Westminster. Stamps marked the opening of the Canberra parliament building in 1927, the pioneer flights of Kingsford Smith in 1931, the Sydney Harbour Bridge in 1932, submarine telephone link in 1936, and the armed forces who held on to part of New Guinea and thwarted the Japanese in 1940. In 1945 the Duke of Gloucester was the last English governor-general.

Australian security after 1945 depended on the USA, recognised by a stamp of the War Memorial at Canberra in 1955. Troops were sent to Korea and Vietnam, and Australia joined SEATO in 1954 and the Asian and Pacific Council in 1966. Decimal currency was adopted, and identity with Asia publicised on three stamps in 1971. The Osaka World Fair issue in the previous year showed the growing trade with Japan. Australia has proved rich in energy and metals (531) as well as farmland (529) and the entry of Britain into Europe in 1973 led to further assertion of independence by the Labour Government whose political roots were in English Chartism.

New Zealand has become an idealised Britain of beautiful scenery and farms. Her industries appeared on the Chambers of Commerce Congress series of 1936, and on definitives after 1960 (534). Her history was traced on the very fine centenary of British sovereignty series of 1940, and in 1965 Wellington was host to the eleventh Commonwealth Parliamentary Conference. In 1968 the seventy-fifth year of universal suffrage was marked, and this and the Human Rights stamp of the same year were printed by the Japanese Government Bureau.

The islands of the South Pacific had no obvious economic benefits, but seemed to fulfil aspirations for Utopia and adventure. John Williams, eaten in 1839, and Bishop C. Patteson, murdered in 1871, stimulated British interest while there was bitter rivalry with France over Pritchard's imprisonment in Tahiti in 1843 (537). Britain had refused to grant protectorate. Gauguin's paintings preserve the pagan beauty, which European morals and diseases destroyed rapidly, though there was time for scientific study of the culture. Pitcairn was a colony from 1790 when *The Bounty* mutinied: stamps have financed it since 1940. Fiji issued typed stamps in 1870, the arms of King Cakobau in 1871, and became a colony in 1874, followed by Christmas in 1888 (which issued stamps from 1958 for the nuclear test staff), Gilbert and Ellice 1892, the Solomons 1893 and Tonga in 1900. George I and II had stamps printed in Wellington from 1886. The joint control of the New Hebrides in 1906 showed that Britain and France had at last come to realise that there were more important issues than colonies.

Germany had annexed her share of the islands, and a powerful cruiser squadron wrought havoc in 1914, defeating a British force at Coronel, but was itself obliterated in

PLATE 49
Australia and New Zealand

Australia
528 1932 kookaburra: the unique fauna have featured on most definitive issues.
529 1953: three se-tenant designs publicised primary industries.
530 1957: honouring the famous and essential 'Flying Doctor' service
531 1970: the development of natural resources for the expansion of industry

New Zealand
532 1946: the Parliament Building, Wellington, in the long peace series
533 1935: Maori girl
534 1967: decimal currency on 1960 design of flora and industries
535 1971: health, an annual charity series introduced in 1930.

PLATE 49

528

529

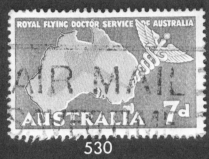

530

531

532

533

534

535

1915 in the Falkland Islands. Japan gained control of the Marshall and Caroline islands belying the name 'Pacific' by her conquests in 1941–2.

These gains did not include the Ellices or Midway: the death of Yamamoto in 1943 over the Solomons, and USA landings on the Gilberts, were the turning point in the Pacific war. There were occupation stamps only in Malaya (475).

Many territories have populations less than towns, and distances are too great for federation. Nevertheless independence has been granted, to Western Samoa 1962, the Cook Islands 1965, Nauru 1968 and Fiji 1970, where a university was founded in 1969. Very close links are maintained with the former rulers. Since the nuclear test-ban treaty of 1963, only the French have disturbed the peace of the region with new tests in 1973.

The frozen land-mass round the South Pole is one of the remaining untapped resources of the world. Britain began seal hunting in 1778 and issued stamps for four dependencies of the Falkland Islands in 1944. Norway first reached the pole in 1911—France, Australia, and New Zealand, issuing stamps since 1957, claim territory. Nine other countries set up bases and in 1961 a treaty guaranteed no military use. Argentine and Chile claim the British area, while the USA, USSR and Japan do not recognise any claims. France issued stamps for islands in the southern Indian Ocean and Antarctica in 1955, and there is a large mail relative to the population.

CONCLUSION

The postage stamp has been an important tool in the age of most rapid human change. This book has only given guidelines to what can be learned from these tiny, but very detailed, documents. No mention has been made of postmarks, which alone distinguished some British post offices and colonies 1857–1900, and which, in the age of the automatic franking machine, provide new areas for collectors. Advertising slogans have provided for local and special interests, and as the increase in pictorial and commemorative issues has stimulated new collectors, there is no likelihood of the now old-fashioned adhesive label being replaced. These will continue to cater for all possible thematic interests, including past history. This may have no relevance to the issuing state at all, as with some art issues, but the most valuable educational function of the stamp will continue to be what it says about the life and politics of its country of origin.

PLATE 50
The South Pacific and the Antarctic

536 Nauru 1924, an Australian mandate of a German colony. A republic since 1968

537 Polynesia 1958, formerly French Oceanic Settlements, which include Tahiti.

538 Fiji 1941, the most populous group in the South Pacific

539 Tonga 1953, the popular Queen Salote 1920–65 of the 'Friendly Islands'

540 Samoa 1966. Independent since 1960 after German and New Zealand control

541 South Georgia: in 1963 the British Antarctic Territories were separated from the Falkland Islands.

542 Australian Antarctic Territory 1961. Stamps issued since 1957 for the area under commonwealth control from 1933.